The Boots Book
of Home Wine Making
and Brewing

The Boots Book of Home Wine Making and Brewing

B. C. A. Turner

Published for the Boots Company Limited

by Wolfe Publishing Ltd.
10 Earlham St. London WC2H 9LP

The author would like to thank the following
for their co-operation in supplying accessories
for the use in photographs:

William Page & Co. Ltd.
Eggomania
Tiddy Dol's Eating House

Photography by Gina Harris and Anthony Kay

Reprinted 1971, 1972, 1973, 1974
New and revised edition 1975, 1976, 1977

Printed by Ebenezer Baylis & Son Ltd
Leicester and London

Contents

List of Illustrations

Metric Conversion Tables

Measurements given throughout this book are Imperial measures. The metric equivalent of all recommended quantities is provided in each case and also below.

Liquid measurements

Liquid measure is common for all flowers and tree berries. You simply use a pint, quart or litre measure, usually a jug, place the flowers or berries in it and press them down lightly.

$\frac{1}{2}$ pint	=	0.284	litres
1 pint	=	0.568	litres
2 pint	=	1.136	litres
3 pint	=	1.704	litres
4 pint	=	2.273	litres
$5\frac{1}{2}$ pint	=	3.125	litres

6 pint	=	3.409	litres
$8\frac{1}{2}$ pint	=	4.830	litres
1 quart	=	1.136	litres
2 quart	=	2.273	litres
3 quart	=	3.409	litres
1 gallon	=	4.546	litres
2 gallon	=	9.092	litres
3 gallon	=	13.638	litres
4 gallon	=	18.184	litres
5 gallon	=	22.730	litres
6 gallon	=	27.276	litres
10 gallon	=	45.460	litres
15 gallon	=	68.189	litres

Solid measurements

$\frac{1}{4}$ oz.	=	7.087	grms
$\frac{1}{2}$ oz.	=	14.175	grms
$\frac{3}{4}$ oz.	=	21.262	grms
1 oz.	=	28.350	grms
$1\frac{1}{4}$ oz.	=	35.437	grms
$1\frac{1}{2}$ oz.	=	42.525	grms
$1\frac{3}{4}$ oz.	=	49.612	grms
2 oz.	=	56.699	grms
3 oz.	=	85.049	grms
4 oz.	=	113.40	grms
6 oz.	=	170.10	grms
8 oz.	=	226.80	grms
12 oz.	=	340.19	grms
$15\frac{1}{2}$ oz.	=	439.41	grms
24 oz.	=	680.39	grms
26 oz.	=	737.09	grms
36 oz.	=	1020.6	grms
$\frac{1}{4}$ lb.	=	113.40	grms

$\frac{1}{2}$ lb.	=	226.80	grms
$\frac{3}{4}$ lb.	=	340.20	grms
1 lb.	=	0.454	krgms
$1\frac{1}{2}$ lb.	=	0.681	krgms
2 lb.	=	0.907	krgms
$2\frac{1}{4}$ lb.	=	1.020	krgms
$2\frac{1}{2}$ lb.	=	1.134	krgms
$2\frac{3}{4}$ lb.	=	1.247	krgms
3 lb.	=	1.361	krgms
$3\frac{1}{2}$ lb.	=	1.588	krgms
4 lb.	=	1.814	krgms
$4\frac{1}{2}$ lb.	=	2.041	krgms
5 lb.	=	2.268	kgrms
6 lb.	=	2.722	kgrms
8 lb.	=	3.629	kgrms
10 lb.	=	4.536	kgrms
12 lb.	=	5.443	kgrms
15 lb.	=	6.804	kgrms
20 lb.	=	9.072	kgrms

Temperatures

40°F = 4.4°C	65°F = 18.3°C
45°F = 7.2°C	70°F = 21.1°C
50°F = 10°C	75°F = 23.9°C
59°F = 15°C	145°F = 62.8°C
	150°F = 65.6°C

Dried and Fresh Fruit Comparison Table

Dried fruit	Sugar content	Fresh fruit equivalent (Multiply weight of dried fruit by)	Water content fresh fruit	Carbo-hydrate content
Currants Raisins Sultanas	66.5%	4	81.5%	17.3%
Apples	54%	6	84.8%	14.1%
Apricots	46.5%	$5\frac{1}{2}$	85.3%	12.8%
Bananas	65%	3	75.7%	22.2%
Figs	56.5%	$3\frac{1}{2}$	77.5%	20.3%
Peaches	43.4%	$5\frac{1}{2}$	89.1%	9.7%
Pears	39.5%	3	83.2%	15.3%
Prunes	44%	4	82.1%	16.6%
Bilberries	18.5%	$4\frac{1}{2}$	83.2%	15.3%
Elderberries	15%	4	79.8%	16.4%

As an example : 1 lb of dried currants equals 4 lbs of fresh.

NOTE : Since the quality of fruit varies so much from variety to variety, from place to place and from year to year, the above figures are averages. They nevertheless give a valuable guide to the relative contents of popular dried and fresh fruits.

Note on the use of Campden Tablets
When Campden tablets are listed with the ingredients, the quantity usually one, must be used in accordance with instructions in the making of wine. There are, however, occasions during preparation, racking and fermentation when additional Campden tablets may be required, but these do not form part of the recipe and quantities are not listed with the ingredients.

Introduction

The craft of making wine and beer is maybe ten thousand years old. Different kinds are made in almost every part of the inhabited earth. Since 1945 there has been a tremendous upsurge, especially but not exclusively in Great Britain, Canada, the U S A, South Africa, Australia and New Zealand.

There is now an extensive and comprehensive range of equipment and ingredients available so that the needs of newcomers to wine and beer making are easily met. This book will show you in words and pictures, just how to make palatable wine as good as the best "vin ordinaire". Home brewers, too, will quickly realise that they can readily make beer as good as the best they can buy.

Whether you are a beginner, the proud possessor of a kit with a few samples to your credit, or even a regular summer fruit enthusiast, this book will help you. You will see that it is set out clearly and simply in an easy-to-follow way, and technical words have been avoided or simplified wherever possible.

Because it is so clearly set out, you can the more easily refresh your mind on the bits you know and concentrate on the problems troubling you. You will find recipes and techniques for using jams, syrups, tinned and dried fruit and so on.

Wines and beers out of season as it were, or — if you prefer — just when it suits you.

Attention!

You are strongly recommended to read through the following pages before attempting any of the recipes for the first time. You will then make your wine with a clearer understanding of the methods and a consequent improvement in the quality.

All recipes make 6 bottles of wine unless stated otherwise. To make more, increase quantities of all ingredients pro rata except yeast, which need not be increased at all.

Quantities are given in Imperial and metric measures. They do not always equate precisely, but will nevertheless produce very similar wines. In home wine-making quantities are not critical and minor variations may be safely made. The variations in the quality of basic ingredients are such that no two wines are ever likely to be exactly the same.

The specific gravity of grape juice concentrate varies from manufacturer to manufacturer and the recipes are based on an average concentrate.

The ingredients have been balanced in each recipe in both Imperial and metric, which accounts for the occasional variations in conversion. For example, in the recipe for Brown Ale only 450 grams of sugar are equated with 1 lb, but in the same recipe 1 kg of malt extract is equated with 2 lb. The ultimate carbohydrate quantity will be similar in both Imperial and metric. Variations of this kind are not cause for concern.

All quantities of water in the recipes are approximate because sugar and fruits create a certain amount of liquid which it is not always easy to calculate precisely.

Vocabulary

Acid

Essential for fermentation. Citric, tartaric or malic acid may be used. Dry wines need to contain about 4 to 5 parts per thousand, sweet wines from 6 to 7. Acetic acid is the vinegar taste — to be avoided.

Air-Lock

Sometimes also called a fermentation lock. It is a device used during fermentation to exclude air whilst permitting carbon dioxide to escape.

Alcohol

The intoxicating spirit formed during fermentation which gives wine its characteristic flavour and satisfaction.

Body

The fullness of wine.

Campden Tablet

The trade name for a small tablet of potassium metabisulphite which releases 50 parts per million of sulphur dioxide when dissolved in water or wine. The sulphur sterilises equipment, prevents the growth of moulds, bacteria and spoilage yeasts and improves the flavour of the wine.

Carbon Dioxide

The gas formed during fermentation. It can be seen escaping in bubbles and be heard as a hissing sound made by the bursting of the bubbles when they reach the surface. Almost half the sugar is converted into alcohol and half into carbon dioxide thus 2 lb 3 oz (1 kg) of sugar will produce 1 lb $\frac{1}{2}$ oz (approx 470 grams) of carbon dioxide gas and 1 lb 1 oz (480 grams) of alcohol.

Decant

To pour clear wine from a bottle in which a sediment has been formed into a glass vessel suitable for use at the table. The bottle is held to the light and tipped carefully so that clear wine slides slowly into the decanter. As the sediment nears the neck of the bottle pouring is stopped.

Dry

A term used to describe a wine in which there is no residual sugar.

Enzyme

Molecules of protein joined to an organic compound which acts as a catalyst in specific circumstances. Many different enzymes are necessary in winemaking. They are secreted by the yeast cells and by their very presence cause changes in the substances around them. They are not changed themselves. Each different enzyme is effective in only one change. For example invertase causes sucrose to separate into glucose and fructose. It cannot cause any further changes. A different enzyme is responsible for each of the many complicated changes in the long process of the conversion of sugar into alcohol and carbon dioxide.

Fermentation

The process of converting sugar in a must or wort into alcohol and carbon dioxide. It is caused by enzymes secreted in the yeast cells.

Filtration

The removal of minute solid particles suspended in a wine, by passing it through a filter kit.

Fining

The removal of minute particles suspended in a wine by the addition of wine finings such as isinglass or bentonite. As the finings sink to the bottom they attract to themselves the solid particles and carry them down to form a sediment from which the clear wine can be racked.

Fortification

The adding of alcohol to a wine so as to increase its strength. Usually only Vodka or Polish spirit are used since they do not affect the flavour of the wine.

Hydrometer

An instrument for measuring the specific gravity of a liquid. In winemaking this indicates the quantity of sugar in a given liquid. (See p. 26).

14

Invert Sugar	A mixture of fructose and glucose produced from sucrose – ordinary sugar in the form that it is bought every day. It is used in brewing to ensure a speedy fermentation.
Lees	The dross or sediment consisting of dead yeast cells, dust, fruit pulp, etc., etc., which falls to the bottom in fermentation and storage vessels as wines fall bright.
Macerate	Describes the action of bruising flower petals.
Maturation	The ageing of a wine to the point at which it is most pleasant to drink.
Must	The name given to liquid before it is fermented into wine.
Nutrient	Nitrogenous matter essential for yeast growth. Usually bought in the form of a prepared tablet containing di-ammonium phosphate or the like.
Pectolytic Enzyme	A compound which breaks down the pectin in fruit, thus increasing the extraction of the juice and clarity of the wine.
Proof	A liquid that is "Proof" contains 57.1% alcohol by volume. 70° Proof means that the liquid contains 70% of 57.1% i.e. 40% alcohol.
Racking	A process of transferring clear or clearing wine from jars containing lees or sediment into clean jars. Usually performed with the aid of a siphon.
Sediment	Another name for lees.
Siphon	In its simplest form no more than a rubber tube through which a clear wine can be conveyed from a jar containing sediment into a clean jar.
Specific Gravity	The weight of a given volume of liquid compared with

the same volume of water at 15°C (59°F). Used in wine-making to measure the amount of sugar in a liquid.

Starter Bottle

A bottle containing a fruit juice including acid, nutrient, sugar and water at a temperature of 23.9°C (75°F), together with yeast. The yeast is activated and begins the process of fermentation so that when the contents of the bottle are added to the must fermentation begins without delay.

Sulphite

The short name for potassium or sodium metabisulphite from which sulphur dioxide is released in solution. See also Campden tablet.

Sweet

A wine which contains some residual sugar after fermentation. The opposite of dry.

Tannin

A bitter substance which gives "bite" and slight astringency to wine. Essential in a well balanced wine.

Thin

The term used to describe a wine that lacks substance and has a watery consistency. The opposite of a wine with plenty of body.

Wort

A liquid containing a solution of malt and hop essence before fermentation into beer.

Yeast

Microscopic botanical cells which secrete enzymes that cause fermentation by the reduction of sugar to alcohol and carbon dioxide. Wine and beer yeasts are called saccharomyces, which means sugar fungi. Yeast is essential to the making of a wine or beer.

A note on yeasts recommended in this book
G.P. YEAST means a General Purpose Yeast such as Boots' Wine Yeast Compound, Unican 'Super Yeast' and C.W.E. 'Formula 67' suitable for most table wines. G.P. Yeast may be used instead of the named varieties if you so wish.

What is Wine?

The Shorter Oxford English Dictionary gives several definitions of wine. It is described firstly, as the fermented juice of the grape and secondly, as a fermented liquor made from the juice of other fruits or from grain, flowers, the sap of various trees and so on.

The Wine Trade tends to deprecate home-made wines and would certainly prefer the word wine to mean only the product of the fermentation of freshly pressed grape juice. But right is on our side and you are perfectly correct in calling your fermented beverage apple wine or plum wine or whatever the ingredient may be.

The chief ingredients of wine are water, flavouring, sugar, acid, tannin and, of course, alcohol. The alcohol is formed from the sugar during fermentation. Fermentation is caused by the microscopic vegetable cell, called yeast. Whatever else you may have heard or whatever recipes you may have seen, wine cannot be made without yeast. Some fruits, notably the grape, have an abundance of suitable yeast on their skin. In Britain it is described as "bloom" and looks like a whitish powder; it is particularly noticeable on plums. Most fruits, flowers, vegetables, cereals and certainly tinned or bottled juices and concentrates have no yeast on them and a suitable yeast *must* be added to ensure an adequate fermentation. Yeast is the key to making a good wine and will be described more fully later on, but enough now to say that the yeast causes the sugar to change into alcohol in a process called fermentation and this is what makes wine so different and special.

You may still ask "But what is wine?" "Why all the fuss? What does wine look like, smell like and taste like?" "What does it do for me?" Throughout the centuries poets have been asking these questions, describing wine as the nectar of the gods, as the joy of man's heart, as solace, as merriment, as medicine. There is no end.

In appearance a glass of wine is red, white, rosé or tawny. The red can range like a rose, from almost black to vermilion. White includes every subtle hue of yellow, from the colourless water almost to green. Similarly with rosé and tawny, there is a wide range of the basic colour. Good wine is bright and clear with a fresh, clean smell, sometimes fruity, sometimes vinous.

In the mouth, wine tastes crisp and again clean and fresh. It may taste strong and robust or light of texture. The taste of the fresh juice from which it was made is no longer pronounced. It may taste dry or sweet but always balanced so that you are not aware of the acid, the tannin, the alcohol or of any of the ingredients.

Wine has great medicinal benefits. In past centuries extracts from herbs were mixed with it, to alleviate different ailments. Wounds were washed in wine to clean them and aid their healing. Even today it is recommended as a tonic after illness.

In addition to being pleasing to the eye, nose, palate, and, indeed, the whole being, wine is good for you. Need one say more !

Why Make Your Own Wine?

Most people probably make wine because it is so much cheaper than buying it. Of this there is no doubt. It is perfectly easy to make for a few pence wine as good as that which costs ten or fifteen times as much.

But this is not the only reason. It is a creative hobby with an admirable end product. It satisfies the desire to make something entire. So many jobs in life are only part of a whole and, often, such a small part as to seem insignificant. In making wine you satisfy your desire to make something complete and whole, from start to finish.

It is a hobby too, that can be followed indoors, even in the smallest flat at any time of the year. It is simple to do, requires no training nor special expertise. The equipment is simple and cheap and nowadays easy to acquire. Ingredients are available everywhere and are frequently part of the household stock.

But it is also a hobby with extensions. It can be associated with keeping bees, growing fruits, with country walks. It can be associated with other people in the form of wine-making clubs that flourish almost everywhere − clubs in which you can compare your wine with others and learn from other people's mistakes. It can be associated with exhibiting at horticultural shows and the glory of winning trophies for making the best wine in the show.

Winemaking is a gregarious and friendly hobby. It engenders friendship. It ensures many happy evenings drinking wine and, above all, talking about wine.

Of one thing you can be sure, that making your own not only enables you to drink far more wine than you could possibly afford to buy, but also provides you with an enjoyable and satisfying hobby, that is guaranteed to bring you years of happiness amongst new friends who

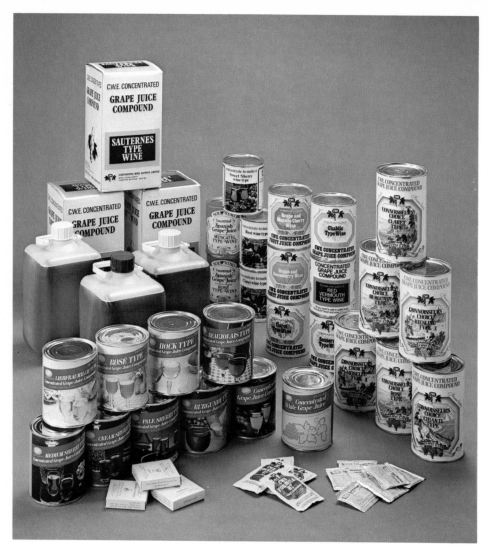

A wide selection of different grape juice concentrates and yeasts.

All you need to start making wine at home.

share your interests.

For the blossoming adolescent a little knowledge of wine is the beginning of education for a civilised way of living. For the newly married, burdened with a mortgage, a baby, bills and a boss, wine brings hope for better days and contentment with the present.

For the middle aged, flagging in the rat race, wine reduces tension, aids digestion, restores ego and makes life worthwhile.

For the elderly, wine engenders warmth and comfort. It brings back happy memories and sets a rosy filter in the spectacles of disillusion.

Your own wine adds to all these gifts the satisfaction of creation, and brings you a little nearer to the mystery of life.

Make your own wine then, for your own sake.

When to Make Wine

Until recently the time to make wine was when the fruit was ripe, the flowers in bloom or the vegetables at their best. The summer and autumn were hectic months and frequently facilities were strained to the utmost. Happily, the situation has now changed. It is true that the fruit, flowers and vegetables still crop at the same times of year, but with so much dried, tinned and frozen fruit, fruit juice concentrates and jams available, we can now spread our winemaking evenly over the whole year.

Winter wines are just as good as the summer wines. They are sound, clean, well-flavoured, and may be enjoyed the following winter and its subsequent summer.

It is always the right time to make wine, even if there is snow on the ground! Frequently the winter evenings and weekends are when we have the most time to spare.

Wine can be made every day in the year and there is nearly always some racking or bottling to do of young wines in bulk storage.

In recent years the varieties of grape juice concentrate have increased and the quality improved enormously. Excellent wine can now be made every day of the year from a can of concentrated grape juice. Some have fruit juices added to them and many are blended to produce wines of a particular type. Whether you fancy sweet or dry, red, white or rosé, or something quite different, there is now a can to suit your palate.

Try Boots' own concentrates for excellence with economy. C.W.E., Solvino and Unican for experiment and variety.

You can't go wrong.

Winemaking is simplicity itself.

You have to take elementary precautions against spoilage by observing a few simple rules of hygiene. These will be fully discussed in their place, but sufficient here to note that all equipment must be kept clean and the wine must be kept covered in all its stages to keep out spoilage organisms such as the vinegar fly.

Winemaking divides itself naturally into three parts:

1 Preparation

The basic ingredients are picked from their stalks, washed, stoned, cut up, crushed, boiled or whatever may be necessary. Water is added and usually 1 or 2 Campden tablets to each gallon (5 litres) to inhibit mould growth and prevent oxidation. In fruit wines a pectolytic enzyme is also added to assist in juice and flavour extraction and subsequent clarity in the finished wine. Acid and tannin are added to make up for their insufficiency in the base ingredients.

Recipes on cans of concentrates should be carefully followed step by step.

Use only natural polythene, glass, stainless steel or ceramic containers. Avoid iron, brass, copper, galvanised iron, lead, glazed earthenware or chipped enamel vessels. The acids in the must react with the metal to form salts that can be poisonous. After adding a Campden tablet always allow 24 hours to pass before adding the nutrient and yeast.

The fruit pulp and liquid prior to fermentation is called must and should always be kept covered to keep it clean and free from spoilage bacteria. A sheet of polythene film spread over the top of your vessel and secured with a rubber band or tied down with a piece of string makes an excellent cover.

Leave the vessel in a warm place for 24 hours for the Campden tablet and pectolytic enzyme to become effective.

2 Fermentation

Next day the sugar, nutrient and an activated yeast are added. The vessel is re-covered and left in the warm. The yeast causes the sugar to split into almost equal parts by weight of alcohol and an invisible and odourless gas called carbon dioxide rises to the surface in bubbles and bursts with a hissing noise. Within a day or so a vigorous ferment will occur. Fruit must be pressed down twice a day to keep it in the liquid and prevent it from drying out and becoming the home for spoilage organisms. If a wine from a concentrate is being made, the must should be placed in a fermentation jar fitted with an air-lock. Some headroom should be left for any foaming that may occur.

Fruit wines being fermented in the presence of the crushed fruit should be strained after 4 or 5 days fermentation. The must should then be transferred to a fermentation jar fitted with an air-lock and left in a temperature of 68°F (20°C)

The air-lock is essential not only to keep out dust and bacteria, but also to cut off the oxygen supply to the yeast. This inhibits further reproduction by the yeast and prevents the formation of a yeasty smell and taste due to an excess of yeast cells.

Maintain a warm temperature around the jar until fermentation is complete or until you wish to stop it so that you finish with a sweet wine not too strong in alcohol. When fermentation stops of its own accord, no more bubbles of gas pass through the air-lock. It can be checked by using an hydrometer. For a dry wine the reading should be S.G. 0.996 or thereabouts.

3 Maturation

Fermentation usually takes only a few weeks, but can last up to 6 months. When it is finished, move the jar to a cool place and leave for a few days for the sediment to settle and the wine to clear.

Pour or preferably siphon the young wine off the sedi-ment into a clean jar that has been sterilised by rinsing it with a sulphite solution. Drain out the sulphite and im-mediately pour in the new wine. It is a good habit always to add a crushed Campden tablet to each jar of wine to stabilise the wine and protect it from infection.

The process of siphoning the wine from the sediment is known as racking and should be carried out whenever a firm deposit is formed. This removes the dead yeast cells before they decompose and taint the wine with an off flavour.

Sometimes a wine will not clear naturally or quickly enough and then wine finings have to be added or the wine has to be filtered. It is best to rack a wine before attempting to filter it, since the sediment would quickly clog the filter. Wines that you wish to finish sweet could always be filtered after the first racking and the addition of 2 Campden tablets. During maturation rough tastes will be smoothed and the wine will improve in bouquet and flavour. This period needs great patience. Home-made wine is so often drunk before it has matured properly. Most of our wines – especially the reds – need at least six months' storage in jar and a further six months in bottle. Very few wines made in the home taste as good in their first year as they do in their second and third years. But they are so well worth waiting for.

A note on the use of the hydrometer

The hydrometer in general use is not a 100% precise instrument: Furthermore, when sugar is added to a wine must other factors may affect the reading slightly especially at the lower and upper ends of the scale.

Therefore examples in this book are given more to emphasise the need to use an hydrometer than to indicate accurate measurements. The author believes his recommended approximations to be thoroughly effective.

The Equipment Required

As in every hobby, you can make a start with a few simple pieces of equipment and increase your range with experience. A fairly comprehensive list is given, from which you can make your selection. The items are listed in the order in which you are likely to use them.

Preparation

1   Polythene bucket with lid approximately two gallons or about 9 litres. Polythene bin with a lid approximately 5½ gallons or about 25 litres. Polythene bin with lid approximately 15 gallons or about 70 litres. Alternatively a salt glazed earthenware crock may be used or an oak tub. These are both very heavy, however, and the tub is difficult to keep clean. If lids are not available, several thicknesses of linen cloth or a sheet of polythene should be used to keep out dust and dirt.

2   A fruit crusher. A piece of oak or boxwood on the end of a broom handle is excellent.

3   A fruit press. This is essential for large quantities of fruit. It should be used in conjunction with a linen bag which is in any case needed for pressing small quantities of fruit by hand. A juice extractor may be used if one is possessed.

4   A strong, long handled wooden or plastic spoon.

5   Polythene funnels. You need one that is 2½″ (6 cm) in diameter for filling bottles and one that is 5″ (12 cm) in diameter for filling jars.

6   Hydrometer and trial jar. Very well worth having if you want to control the alcohol content and sweetness of your wine. It is essential to the serious winemaker.

Fermentation

1   Fermentation jars. A glass demijohn is best. Usually it holds a little more than a gallon, about 8½ pints or

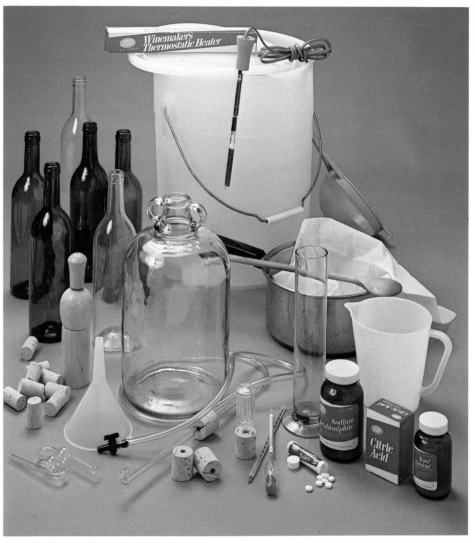

Equipment for making wine. Note the natural polythene mashing bin, jug and funnel.

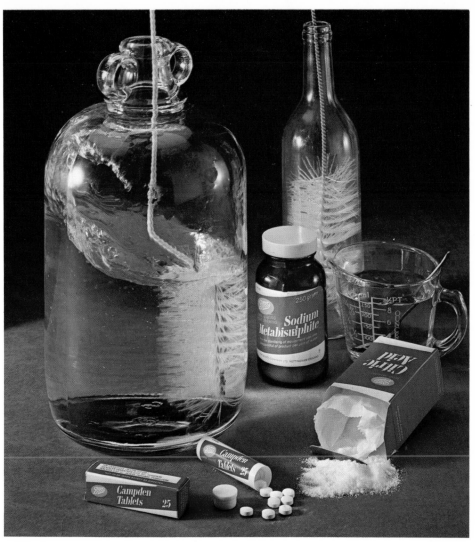

Essential brushes for cleaning jars and bottles. Note the sterilising solution prepared from metabisulphite and citric acid.

approximately 5 litres.

2   Supply of air-locks and bored corks to fit the demijohns. Glass air-locks indicate the activity of fermentation best, but being glass they are fragile and break easily. The plastic "handy fermentation lock" is much cheaper but just as effective though less interesting to watch. In the absence of any such lock a plug of cotton wool may be used.

Maturation

1   Siphon. Transparent plastic siphon tubing alone will do but a siphon pump is worth having.

2   Storage jars are necessary. Large demijohns may be used with safety but remember their fragility. Earthenware storage jars whilst a little heavier keep out the light and help to stabilise the temperature. Oak wine casks of at least five gallon capacity (22 litres) may be used in conjunction with a stand so that they can be stored on their sides. Please note that old vinegar casks should never be used in any circumstances. High density polythene vessels may be used for short periods but are not recommended for long term use.

3   Good tight fitting bungs are most important.

4   A supply of wine bottles of the 26⅔ oz (750 cc) size is essential. Do not use screw stoppered or even spirit bottles. Apart from their poor appearance they are thin and dangerous. The same is true of squash and sauce bottles. Use dark wine bottles for red wine and clear bottles for white wine. Champagne bottles are absolutely essential for sparkling wines.

5   A bottle brush helps to clean bottles and jars easily and effectively – in the punt and under the shoulder!

6   Straight wine corks are better than cork stoppers, they are longer and enable the bottles to be stored on their sides.
This keeps them moist and swollen and tighter fitting.

7   A hand corking machine will be found most useful when you are using the straight sided corks, particularly when you have a good number of bottles to cork.

8   Plastic or metal foil bottle caps cover the cork and neck of the bottle and give a professional appearance. Always use them when you give a bottle of wine to a friend.

9   Decorative labels are important too, not only for giving information about the contents but also for improving the appearance of the finished bottle.

10 A wine rack will be an asset to the enthusiast. The bottles can be stored properly on their sides.

Sulphite is essential in keeping equipment clean and sterile. Although it is also used as an ingredient, it is an essential to ensure perfect cleanliness of every utensil used. It is most commonly available in the form of Campden tablets but can also be bought in the form of a crystalline powder called sodium metabisulphite. One tablet and a few grains of citric acid dissolved in one pint of cold water makes an ideal destroyer of bacteria and fungi (or two or more tablets when citric acid is not used). The solution gives off a gas called sulphur dioxide, long known for its purifying properties. Do not use hot water, since the heat releases the gas too quickly, before it has time to sterilise the utensils.

The Ingredients Needed

The immense variety of fresh or dried fruits, canned or pulped fruits, jams, jellies and juices, grape concentrate, flowers, vegetables, cereals and honey will be mentioned in the recipes with details for preparing each one. Mention will be made here, however, of the other ingredients which are common to nearly all wines:

1 Sugar

Undoubtedly the ordinary white granulated sugar is best. Cheapest to buy, easiest to handle, without flavour and of the same chemical compound as other sugars. It can be used in crystal form, or better still dissolved in hot water to form a syrup. 2 lb (1 kg) of sugar gently boiled for twenty minutes in one pint ($\frac{1}{2}$ litre) of water containing a teaspoonful of citric acid, will produce an inverted sugar that can be fermented immediately it is cool. Ordinary sugar is a combination of fructose and glucose. Before fermentation starts the combination has to be split into its two component parts; this is usually done by an enzyme secreted by the yeast, called invertase. Boiling the sugar with citric acid or lemon juice has the same effect and so we call such a syrup invert sugar. Demerara, brown sugar, Barbados sugar and the like MAY be used but they impart a flavour of caramel or burnt sugar to a greater or lesser degree. Whilst they are not recommended for delicate wines they may be used effectively when making Madeira type wines with a Madeira yeast.

Fructose and glucose may be used instead of sucrose when this is difficult to obtain. Honey or commercially inverted sugar may also be used but to allow for the water content, 20% more has to be used than of dry granulated sugar. Sugar cubes, caster sugar and icing sugar may all be used but should be dissolved in warm water and added in syrup form. Golden syrup or treacle may used especially for red dessert wines. Since the specific gravity will vary, it is best to dissolve the treacle in warm water and when cool check the S G . You are likely to need 25% or so more than dry sugar. Dark and black treacle must be avoided at all costs since they impart a most distinctive and unpleasant taste to the wine.

A little saccharin or tablets such as Sweetex, may be used to sweeten a finished wine. Start off with 3 tablets to the bottle and increase as required. Sweetening that does not consist of carbohydrate is not suitable for fermentation.

2 Acid

Yeast is a tiny vegetable cell that needs an acid solution in which to develop and thrive. Most of our English fruits are so acid that they need dilution, but flowers, cereals, vegetables, honey and even sometmies such fruits as dates contain practically no acid at all. Acid must therefore be added to all wines made from these ingredients. The commonest acids are citric, tartaric and malic. Citric acid is available in oranges, lemons, grapefruits and the like. Tartaric acid is in grapes. Malic acid is in apples. Each has its own merits. Citric acid aids a rapid fermentation, tartaric acid precipitates in alcohol and so reduces the acidity of a wine; malic aids the final flavour by being converted in a subsequent fermentation to lactic acid which is less sharp in flavour than the others. Some winemakers recommend the addition of a blending of all three. This can often best be achieved by adding fresh grapes, grape juice concentrate or dried grapes in the form of raisins or sultanas, to the must. At the very least, each must should have sufficient acid to ensure a good fermentation and a balanced wine; 5 parts per thousand for a dry wine and 7 parts per thousand for a sweet wine is the accepted norm.

3 Nutrient

The yeast cell, like all other vegetable cells, needs nitrogen as well as oxygen to enable it to grow and thrive. Fresh fruits contain nitrogen, though it is greatly diluted by the added water. To enable the yeast to develop well and create sufficient enzymes for the complicated process of fermentation, it is always as well to add some nutrient to every must. This does more than anything else to produce a sound dry wine. Nutrient is best added in the form of white crystals called di-ammonium phosphate. A little less than $\frac{1}{2}$ a level teaspoonful is sufficient for a full gallon jar or 5 litres, but follow the manufacturer's instructions if a different quantity is recommended.

4 Tannin

This is a substance that gives bite to a wine. Without it wine tastes soft and flabby, which is often true of white wines. With too much tannin the wine tastes hard and rough as do some red wines. Tannin is found naturally in grape skins, stones and stalks, in pear and apple skins and in skins of elderberry, damsons, blackberries, red plums and so on. It is also in tea. Musts that are deficient in tannin need some added to them. Half a level teaspoonful of grape tannin powder is sufficient for one gallon or 5 litres of wine.

5 Pectolytic Enzyme

Pectin destroying enzyme breaks down the pectin content of fruit and thus improves the extraction of both juice and flavour. Left in the wine the pectin could cause a haze which would detract considerably from its appearance. Most winemakers add a small quantity as a matter of course to their must. This is desirable rather than essential, but is particularly necessary for stone fruits such as apricot, damson, peach and plum. Pectin destroying enzymes are most effective in a warm must that contains little or no sugar. It is best to use them right at the start, before sugar is added. A teaspoonful per gallon (5 litres) is plenty for most ingredients, but for fruits rich in pectin a table-spoonful is necessary. Supplies vary, however, and should be used as directed by the manufacturer.

6 Sulphite

Sometimes described as the winemaker's best friend, already mentioned under Equipment for its value in

34

sterilising jars, bottles, corks and everything else. Sulphite in the form of Campden tablets or the white crystalline powder — sodium metabisulphite — is of equal value in preventing the growth of bacteria and moulds in must and finished wine. One Campden tablet per gallon or 5 litres, when specified, should always be added right at the start, but yeast must never be added until at least 24 hours later or it will be inhibited!

After racking, 2 Campden tablets should be added to sweet wines, since this stabilises the wine and prevents further fermentation. Dry wines need only one.

Sulphite is also an excellent anti-oxidiser. All fruits start to go brown through oxidation soon after they are crushed. Without proper care this can cause an off flavour in the finished wine. Oxidation is particularly noticeable with apples and pears. Some varieties start to go brown as soon as they are cut so it is important to prepare a vessel containing cold water, one Campden tablet per gallon or 5 litres with a few grains of citric acid crystals and a tea-spoonful of pectic enzyme. The fruit can be put into this as soon as it is cut or crushed. It will then remain white so that only its good flavour is extracted. Sulphite is also the prescribed medicine for a few wine ailments. Never be without plenty of Campden tablets, or loose sulphite. Remember, however, that it is always most effective in cold water with a few grains of citric acid. Dissolve 1 level teaspoonful of sodium or potassium metabisulphite in $\frac{1}{2}$ pint (approx $\frac{1}{4}$ litre) of cool water and $\frac{1}{2}$ teaspoonful of citric acid in a similar quantity of water. Mix the two solutions together and you have a pint (about $\frac{1}{2}$ litre) of a solution suitable for sterilising jars, bottles, corks, siphons, funnels, pressing cloths, spoons and equipment of all kind.

7 Water

The water that comes out of the taps in Great Britain is usually of a very high purity and is perfectly suitable for making wine. Spring water is good too, but well water may need to be boiled. Rain water must be filtered as well as boiled, since it contains so many impurities from the

a. **Assorted sugars**

b. Making an invert sugar solution
2 lb (1 kg) granulated sugar, 1 pint (3/5 litre)
water, 1 tsp. citric acid.

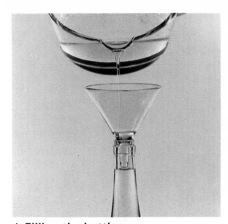

d. Filling the bottle
2 pints (1 litre) equals 2lbs (1 kg) sugar.

c. Boiling the sugar, acid and water

atmosphere. Cold water is recommended for use with strongly flavoured fruits for fermentation on the pulp. It is also recommended for flower wines to avoid the dissipation of the delicate bouquet. On the other hand boiling water poured over gooseberries or plums and the like, not only assists with the purification of the fruit but also softens it, so that when cool it can be easily squashed in your hands.

Boiling vegetables is obviously necessary but fruit should rarely be boiled, since a hazy wine often results.

8 Yeast

The most important ingredient in making wine is yeast. Yeast is a tiny vegetable cell about 8/1000ths of a centimetre long and 7/1000ths of a centimetre wide. It is estimated that there could be as many as five hundred million cells in a quarter litre of fermenting wine. They are not visible to the naked eye but when magnified 500 times by a microscope they can be seen quite clearly. Mostly they reproduce by growing a bud which breaks off when mature, or by dividing in two. Normally they take three hours to grow to maturity before reproducing themselves. A cell will reproduce itself 30 times before it dies.

There are thousands of different varieties of yeast but we are concerned only with a very few of them and in particular with wine yeast and beer yeast. For the technically minded the wine yeast is called saccharomyces elipsoideus because it is elliptical in shape and the beer yeast is called saccharomcyes cerevisiae after the old Roman word for beer. Saccharomyces simply means "sugar fungi".

It is most important always to use a good yeast when making wine, for the following reasons:
1   Wine yeast imparts a good flavour to the wine.
2   After fermentation it sinks to the bottom of the jar and packs firmly together, so that the clear wine can be siphoned off fairly easily.
3   It is able to resist a higher concentration of sulphur dioxide than spoilage organisms, so you can more adequately sterilise your must and so ensure that your

finished wine is pure.

4 Unlike most moulds and fungi, wine yeast needs oxygen for reproduction only. It can live and cause fermentation in the absence of air. This is another reason for excluding air and, therefore, oxygen from the fermentation.

5 Wine yeast has a higher alcoholic tolerance than other yeasts and especially of wild yeasts and spoilage organisms. 10% of alcohol is a desirable minimum for keeping your wine safely.

Selected wine yeasts bearing the name of the region in which they are most common should be used when making wines of a similar kind to their name type, e.g. a Burgundy, a Sauterne, a Champagne, but they will not make a wine similar to their name type irrespective of ingredients or technique. There is a general purpose yeast available which is a mixture of several types and is particularly suitable for making just wine, as opposed to making wine of a particular type.

Saccharomyces cerevisiae already mentioned as the yeast for making beer is the same as that used for making bread. It is sometimes used for making wine as well, but if you do use this yeast it should be in granulated form, because this is free from the contamination of dough and beer. Bread yeast is usually available in the form of a paste and imparts a doughy taste. Brewer's yeast is usually supplied in a cream carton and is strongly flavoured with hops.

Saccharomyces cerevisiae ferments very rapidly producing great clouds of invisible carbon dioxide from a foaming frothy head. That is why it is used in making bread and beer. Its flavour is less good than wine yeast although it can produce nearly as much alcohol. It sometimes settles rather lightly, however, and can be difficult to rack since moving the jar, however carefully, causes the sediment to swirl up into the previously clear wine.

Pressing apple pulp. The whole apples indicate the kind of fruit that may be used. They have to be crushed before pressing.

The Practical Method

Preparing a wine must is not much different from preparing a meal. Firstly you decide what kind of wine you want to make, then you just balance your must accordingly. For example, if you are making a light table wine you will need a smaller quantity of ingredients than for a rich dessert wine.

Ingredients

The best wine is usually prepared from the best ingredients whether they be fresh, dried, canned or concentrated. Other qualities may be used of course, but the results will be relative. In the main, cooking varieties of fruit seem to give the best results. Frequently the flavour of dessert fruits seems to come through increased in pungence when made into wine. This is especially so with gooseberries, strawberries and raspberries.

When the basic ingredients have been selected, they should first be washed and if necessary scrubbed clean from soil, dust, leaves and grass. Vegetables have then to be diced and boiled. Fruits have to be crushed and steeped in water so that the sugar, flavour, acid, tannin and other trace elements can be leached out. Flowers have to be macerated in warm water to extract their perfume, they contain little else of value to the wine. Concentrates like honey, grape juice and other fruit juices only have to be diluted.

Sulphite

If the fruit oxidises it imparts a less pleasant flavour and taste to the wine, so a Campden tablet is added to prevent oxidation. Campden tablets are very hard to crush and slow to dissolve unless they are crushed. A simple way to crush them is to place one in a tablespoon and crush it with the bowl of a teaspoon. This reduces the hard tablet to a powder, which can more easily dissolve in water. Campden tablets should always be added to cold water and never to hot, since this causes the sulphur dioxide gas to escape too quickly. So when hot water is used in the preparation always add Campden tablet and other additives when the water has cooled.

Acid

Since the fruit acid will be diluted with water, and other base ingredients contain no natural acid, it is essential to add some now. Citric, tartaric or malic or a mixture of all three may be used. The recipes indicate average quantities of citric acid; but tests may be made either by titration or by pH papers such as Boots' Indicator Papers for Acidity Testing, to ensure that you add the correct quantity. The natural acid should be checked after dilution but before the addition of nutrient, tannin, sulphite or pectolytic enzyme. A pH reading of between 3.3 and 3.5 is satisfactory, or between 4 and 7 parts per 1,000 upon titration, depending on whether dry or sweet wine is being made. Without sufficient acid wine has a medicinal taste, will not ferment well and will not keep. The acid not only improves the flavour and the fermentation but also assists in protecting the wine from spoilage.

Pectolytic Enzyme

It is a good habit always to add at the same time some pectin destroying enzyme preparation to each gallon (4.5 litres) of must. This assists the juice extraction and prevents pectin haze in the wine. Certain fruits that contain a high quantity of pectin need a larger quantity and this is provided for in the recipes.

Nutrient

When wine is being prepared some nutrient should always be added with the yeast. This can sometimes be omitted in the preparation of sweet wines, providing the wine is being made from fruit, vegetables or concentrates, or if the yeast preparation includes it.

Tannin

Most wines, especially reds, benefit from the addition of a

42

little grape tannin at this stage, half a teaspoonful of the brown grape tannin powder is usually sufficient. Simply shake the powder into a little of the must, stir it into a paste and add it to the whole of the wine. Natural tannin in the fruits is diluted by the addition of water. Honey, flowers, cereals and vegetables don't have any natural tannin anyway.

Mashing

It is usual to put the fruit into the mashing vessel and pour boiling water over it. Then to cover the vessel and leave the fruit to soften and the water to cool before taking any further action. For fruits that oxidise quickly when crushed, however, such as apples and pears, it is best first to put cold water, in which one Campden tablet and a few grains of citric acid have been dissolved, into the vessel. The fruit can then be crushed and dropped at once into this solution and prevent the browning of oxidation.

Additional Ingredients

If a variety of base ingredients are to be used they should all be added at the same time. The best wines contain several different ingredients to produce a balanced must which has the optimum quantities of sugar, acid, tannin, flavour, nutrient, body and so on to produce a good wine.

The must should always be closely covered to keep out dust, moulds and bacteria and should be left in a warm place for 24 hours after the addition of the Campden tablet or metabisulphite.

Before the yeast is added and the second stage is started, the quantity of sugar already in the must should be checked with an hydrometer so that the correct quantity of sugar to be added can be calculated. Naturally the more sugar there is in the fruit, the less need be added from the packet. The measurement and calculations are of the simplest kind.

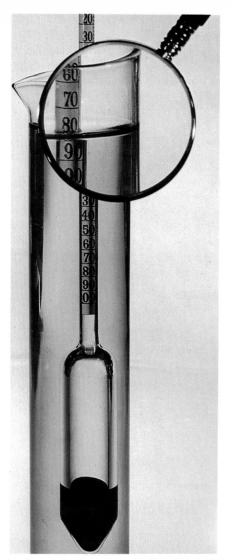

Taking an hydrometer reading S.G. 1.080 is ideal for most table wines.

Preparing a yeast starter bottle
a. Boiled water, lemon juice, sugar, a little malt and of course, yeast.

b. Active yeast ready for use.

It has long been known that the same volume of one substance is heavier or lighter than another. In Great Britain we use an hydrometer to measure the weight of other liquids relative to the weight of the same volume of water. For example, if a gallon (4.5 litres) of water contains 2 lb (1 kg) of sugar dissolved in it, the water will obviously be heavier than plain water without sugar.

If the weight or gravity of a syrupy liquid compared with plain water is as 1.078 to 1.000 we can say that the syrup has a Specific Gravity of 1.078 and we write it as S.G. 1.078 for short.

The standard against which we measure is water at 59°F (15°C). When an hydrometer is placed in a jar of water at this temperature it will float at its scale mark of 1.000. When it is placed in a jar containing some heavier liquid it will float at a higher marking. By a quick reference to the table that follows you can tell at a glance how much sugar is in the liquid. By subtracting this figure from the amount of sugar you want to use to obtain the required amount of alcohol you can tell how much extra sugar to add.

Example 1. You have prepared a must of mixed sweet and cooking apples and raisins and wish to make a table wine of 12% alcohol. After two days you draw off some liquid into your hydrometer jar and place the hydrometer carefully into it. The hydrometer floats, say at 1.030. The tables show that this figure indicates that the must already contains approximately 12 oz (305 grams) of sugar per gallon (4.5 litres) and that you will need approximately 38 oz (1040 grams) of sugar in the gallon (4.5 litres) to achieve 12% alcohol. You therefore need only add 26 oz (38—12=26) (735 grams (1040—305=735)) of sugar in each gallon (4.5 litres) of must.

Example 2. You have prepared a must containing blackberries, raisins, bananas, elderberries and runner beans and wish to make a sweet dessert wine containing about 15½% alcohol. The initial S.G. of the must is say 1.015 equal to 4 oz (120 grams) sugar in the must. But to obtain 15½% alcohol you need 3 lb (1345 grams) sugar in each gallon (4.5 litres) of must and to make the wine sweet you will need a further 6 oz (160 grams). So you must add 3 lb 6 oz—4 oz=3 lb 2 oz (1505—120=1385 grams).

S.G.	Potential per cent alcohol by volume	Amount of sugar in the gallon lb. oz.		Amount of sugar in 4.5 litres grams
1010	0.9		2	60
1015	1.6		4	120
1020	2.3		7	180
1025	3.0		9	245
1030	3.7		12	305
1035	4.4		15	365
1040	5.1	1	1	430
1045	5.8	1	3	490
1050	6.5	1	5	550
1055	7.2	1	7	610
1060	7.8	1	9	670
1065	8.6	1	11	730
1070	9.2	1	13	795
1075	9.9	1	15	855
1080	10.6	2	1	920
1085	11.3	2	4	980
1090	12.0	2	6	1040
1095	12.7	2	8	1100
1100	13.4	2	10	1160
1105	14.1	2	12	1220
1110	14.9	2	14	1285
1115	15.6	3	0	1345
1120	16.3	3	2	1410
1125	17.0	3	4	1470
1130	17.7	3	6	1530
1135	18.4	3	8	1590

Experience will soon show you that it is quicker, easier and more accurate to calculate in S.G. than in pounds, ounces, grams or litres. Simply check the specific gravity of your must and then stir in enough sugar to bring the must up to the specific gravity you require to give the desired amount of alcohol. Most hydrometers indicate the amount of alcohol that can be fermented from the amount of sugar indicated by the specific gravity, but the tables given indicate this even more clearly.

When reading an hydrometer make sure that your eye is on a level with the wine and that you read the scale at the lowest point. The wine becomes saucer shaped in the trial jar and the edges lap higher up the side of the jar and the hydrometer. The illustration on page 44 makes this quite clear.

If the must is warm then adjustment has to be made to the figures as follows:

Temperature in Degrees		Correction to the last figure of the specific Gravity reading.
Centigrade	Farnheit	
10	50	Subtract 0.6
15	59	No correction necessary
20	68	Add 0.9
25	77	Add 2.0
30	86	Add 3.4
35	95	Add 5.0
40	104	Add 6.8

FERMENTATION

This is the function in which the sugar in the must is converted to alcohol and carbon dioxide by the presence of enzymes secreted in the yeast cells.

When the must is fully prepared an active yeast must be added to start the process of fermentation.

Wine yeast comes in several different forms:—
As a tablet sealed in a metal foil.
As a liquid.
As a culture in a sealed test tube.
As granules.
On fragments of dried rose-hip shells.
In these forms the yeast is dormant and takes a little while under ideal conditions to become active. To this end sensible winemakers prepare a starter bottle.

Starter Bottle

To make a starter bottle for a gallon (or 5 litres) of Wine.

a. Assorted Fermentation locks

b. Fermenting a sherry must

c. Close up of a fermentation lock

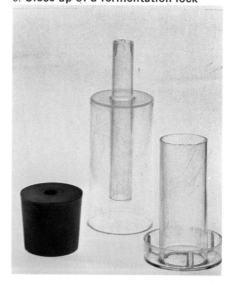

First sterilise a bottle with a sulphite solution, drain it and add about half a pint (a quarter of a litre) of tepid boiled water in which you have dissolved 1 oz (28 grams) of white sugar and a pinch of nutrient. Squeeze out the juice of half an orange and add this to the syrup together with the yeast.

Canned fruit juice may be used instead of water and orange juice, then only half the quantity of sugar is required. Malt extract may also be used but 1 teaspoon is enough and only a quarter of the sugar is needed. BUT don't forget the orange juice or half the quantity of lemon juice.

Shake the bottle well and fit a plug of cotton wool to keep out spoilage bacteria. Stand the bottle in a warm place for up to 48 hours or until you can see plenty of bubbles surging to the surface. The yeast is then vigorously active and may be added to the must so that fermentation can begin without delay.

Half a pint (about a quarter of a litre) is adequate for up to 1 to 3 gallons (14 litres) of must; a pint for 3 to 6 gallons (15 to 27 litres) and a quart for 6 to 10 gallons (28 to 50 litres). The starter should always be fully active and bubbling vigorously.

Air-Lock

If the must is being fermented on the pulp, cover the vessel closely to keep out all dust and dirt, but not so closely that the carbon dioxide gas given off during the fermentation cannot escape. If the must has been strained free from solids and is being fermented in a glass jar or the like, fit an air-lock of the kind illustrated on page 48. Make sure that there is a good seal between the bung and the jar and between the air-lock and the bung. Half fill the air-lock with cold boiled water to which has been added a tiny fraction of a Campden tablet or a pinch of metabisulphite. This will ensure an absolutely sterile lock.

The vessel should now be placed in a warm situation about 70°F or 21 °C, and left to ferment.

You can use the hydrometer not only to find out the quantity of sugar in the must and how much to add, but also to find out how much sugar is left in a wine when fermentation is finished. If the figure is too low the wine may be too dry for you, if it is too high it is probably far too sweet.

Alcohol weighs less than water and so a wine containing alcohol and no residual sugar will have an S.G. below 1.000 perhaps as low as 0.990. A very dry wine will have an S.G. of around 0.990 to 1.000, a medium from 1.002 to 1.008 and a sweet wine will be above 1.010.

By using an hydrometer regularly you can check on the progress of your fermentation, know when your wine is finished and above all control the amount of sugar you use and therefore the amount of alcohol in your wine. In practice it is always advisable to begin fermentation with the must at an S.G. of between 1.080 and 1.085.

If you are planning to make a sweet strong wine, additional sugar should be added in the later stages of fermentation. If too much is added at the beginning, the fermentation sometimes sticks and the wine, of only moderate alcohol content, tastes as sweet as a cordial. Ferment the 1.080 must to say 1.010 then add sugar to raise the S.G. to say 1.025. When it again falls to 1.010 add only enough to raise the S.G. to about 1.016. You may be able to add another dose later, but fermentation will be slowing down and will soon stop. The wine will then be pleasantly sweet and not sickly sweet.

The total alcohol content of such a wine may be calculated as follows :—

Initial S.G. 1.080 fermented to 1.010 equals 70 points. (80–10)

First increase raises S.G. from 1.010 to 1.028 and ferments to 1.010 which equals 18 points. (28–10)

Second increase raises S.G. from 1.010 to 1.027 and ferments to 1.010 which equals 17 points. (27–10)

Third increase raises S.G. from 1.010 to 1.019 and

ferments to 1.010 which equals 9 points. (19–10)
Final reading say 1.010. Total points equals 114.
(70+18+17+9) By referring to the table it will be seen
that 114 points is equal to about $15\frac{1}{2}$% alcohol and this
is the alcoholic content of the wine.

This method is far more satisfactory than any other for
achieving a good fermentation and a strong wine. The
gradual increase in alcohol increases the alcohol tolerance
of the yeast and so produces a strong wine. Furthermore
the yeast is not inhibited by too much sugar at the outset
and gets away to a good start as it were.

If on checking the specific gravity when fermentation
stops, you find that the reading is as low as you expected
it to be, say 1.000, then fermentation has finished. If on
the other hand, the reading seems high, say 1.040, then
the fermentation may have stuck.

Stuck Ferment

There are several causes for this and you must try each
one until you find the answer.

1 Insufficient nutrient and the yeast has died or become
   inhibited. The cure is to add additional nutrient and
   some fresh yeast.
2 Insufficient acid and the yeast has died or become
   inhibited. The cure is to add some extra acid and some
   fresh yeast.

Note: If you start your must with the recommended
quantities of acid, and nutrient, fermentation never ceases
for these reasons. It can stop, however, if you FORGET
to include sufficient acid or nutrient.

3 The must has become too hot and the yeast has
   become inhibited. The cure is to move the jar to a
   cooler position.
4 The must has become too cold and the yeast has
   become inhibited.
   The cure is to move the jar to a warmer place.

Note: With our very changeable weather this can happen
if the must is not in an even temperature situation.
Yeast energiser is often helpful in this situation to get the

(a)

(b)

(c)

Siphoning

a. Suck the wine through the tube.

b. Pinch the end and place it in the jar.

c. This is the minimum difference in height levels. Wine will flow faster with a greater drop.

fermentation moving again.

5   The air-lock may have become clogged and the must so full of carbon dioxide that the yeast has become inhibited. The cure is to pour the wine into a clean jar, allowing the wine to bounce in the centre and so become aerated. Some yeast energiser should be added.

6   If the must has been fermenting vigorously for some time it may be that so much alcohol has been formed that the alcohol tolerance of the yeast has been reached and the yeast is now inhibited from further fermentation. There is no cure, but this situation can be prevented by the wise use of the hydrometer as already indicated.

Autolysis

Yeast cells reproduce very readily under ideal conditions but like all other vegetable cells decomposition eventually sets in. Nitrogen is then released and used by the remaining live yeasts. This process is called autolysis. In the later stages of decomposition unpleasant off flavours are imparted to the wine and it smells and tastes unpleasant. This is why racking is so important in the early stages of maturation.

MATURATION

As soon as fermentation has finished shake the jar and then move it to a cooler place. The dead yeast cells, fruit pulp and other solid materials (known as lees) will slowly fall to the bottom of the jar and the wine will start to clear from the top downwards.

Racking by siphon

After a few days and not more than a week, take the clear wine off the sediment. This is done by standing the jar of wine on a low table and placing a clean jar that has been freshly rinsed with a sulphite solution directly underneath. Remove the air-lock from the jar of wine and insert one end of your siphon into the wine in such a way as not to disturb the lees. Suck or pump the wine through the tube and as soon as the tube is full squeeze it tightly with your thumb and forefinger. This prevents wine from returning to the jar or squirting all over the room. Place the end of the siphon in the clean jar, release the pressure between finger and thumb and allow the wine to flow. Because the length of tube outside the wine jar is longer than the piece inside the jar the amount of wine it contains is greater and therefore heavier. It is this pull of gravity which enables us to siphon off the clear wine so easily. The rule is always to have the empty jar well below the full one.

The end of the siphon in the jar of wine needs some attention. It is important not to allow the sediment to get sucked into the tube and so it is useful either to have a U tube on this end of the siphon or to block up the end and bore some holes in the plastic or rubber tubing, about $\frac{3}{4}''$ (2 cm) from the end. The tube can then be pushed carefully to the bottom of the jar. The U tube sucks wine down into it, thus not disturbing the sediment. The blocked end and bored tube sucks wine in from the sides over the surface of the sediment. A good wine yeast produces a fairly thick and firm sediment which makes siphoning easier. The wrong yeast can produce a flocculent sediment which can be most difficult to rack.

Storage

Campden tablets as suggested on page 35 should be mixed into the wine at the time of the first racking. Finally cork the jar tightly, label it and put it away in a cool dark place, free from vibrations which prevent the wine from clearing. The Campden tablet not only inhibits the growth of bacteria and moulds but also improves the flavour and stabilises the wine by preventing further fermentation.

Always use glass or ceramic jars for storage. Polythene containers sometimes react with the alcohol in the wine and cause an off flavour. They are not suitable for storage purposes, although ideal for the short period of mashing or even fermentation.

Daylight can cause fading of colour and deterioration of flavour, so, if you have no dark cupboard, cover the jars with thick brown paper or a dark cloth.

In this first stage of maturation, it is worth inspecting the wine from time to time, especially if the wine is still cloudy when put away. The act of racking will have encouraged a further deposit to form and the wine should be rapidly clearing until it is star bright. As soon as there is any appreciable deposit to be seen, rack the wine again and at the latest within 8 weeks of having put it away.

Always rack into a clean jar, top up with similar wine or cold boiled water, cork tightly. Store for a further 2 months if it is still cloudy, then rack again at four months if it is clear.

Bottling

After wine has been maturing for nine months or longer and provided it is brilliantly clear, it may be racked into clean bottles. Dark green bottles should be used for red wine and clear glass bottles for white wine. If necessary the bottles should be washed in warm water and scrubbed inside with a bottle brush. Old foil and labels should be removed from the outside. Next rinse the bottles in cold water and finally in a sulphite solution. Stand the bottles upside down to drain for a few minutes and then siphon the matured wine in to the bottles set out on a tray below. Make sure that the wine flows down the inside of the bottle rather than splashing into the centre. Splashing the wine is a harsh treatment, causing diminution of bouquet and an increase in oxidation.

Fill each bottle up to just above the shoulder so that when the cork is inserted there is a gap of not more than $\frac{3}{4}$" (2 cm) between the bottom of the cork and the top of the wine. Allow the bottles to stand for a few minutes so that any bubbles of carbon dioxide which are seen to be rising can burst and escape.

Corking

When the wine is quite still insert the corks. Before doing so however, make sure that they are nice and soft. Always use new corks of the cylindrical variety and the best quality you can obtain. Poor quality corks allow the wine to seep through and the air to enter. As a result the wine will taste

Assorted wine bottles

flat and even vinegarish. Corks soften easily if soaked for a few hours or overnight in a sulphite solution, but care should be taken to ensure that they are kept totally immersed. A basin covered by a saucer suitably weighted is adequate.

Shake off the surplus moisture, insert the cork into the corker, place a piece of plastic covered wire in the neck of the bottle, put the corker onto the bottle and hit the plunger with the heel of your hand or with a mallet. The cork will slide easily into the neck of the bottle and the wire can then be withdrawn allowing the air to escape. With an even air-pressure above and below the cork, it will stay tight. If the plastic covered wire or something similar is not used, the cork may sometimes be forced out a little by the compressed air in the bottle and stand proud.

Dry off the top of the cork with a cloth, then cover the top of the cork and the neck of the bottle with a plastic or foil cap to hide the cork and keep it free from mould.

Labelling

Label the bottle to indicate its contents, being careful to place the label between the two seams and not across one of them.

Finally store the bottle on its side, so that the wine can continue to mature for the next three to nine months or so.

Ailments

Very occasionally something goes wrong when making a wine, no matter how much care has been taken. Happily these occasions are rare, but it is as well to know about them, so that you can the more readily tell the difference between good and bad wine.

Off flavour

The most common fault is an unpleasant flavour, usually caused by insufficient or infrequent rackings. Decomposed yeasts taste and smell like other rotting vegetable matter. The remedy is to siphon clear wine from sediment as often as sediment appears. If the dead yeast is removed from the wine, then it certainly cannot taint it.

Unpleasant flavours can also be caused by using a dirty

utensil or container. Always sterilise every piece of equipment by rinsing it in a sulphite solution before use.

Sometimes the ingredients carry moulds or fungi which spoil flavour. Whenever possible wash ingredients in a sulphite solution and remember to add one Campden tablet or its equivalent to a jar of must or wine, both at the preparation stage and again after fermentation.

Vinegary flavour

The next most common ailment is vinegar taste in the wine. This is due to infection by mycoderma aceti. It floats invisibly in the air and is often carried by the tiny fruit fly seen swarming around decaying fruit. The prevention is simple and effective — always keep fruit, must and wine under an adequate cover, with a close fitting plastic lid, a thick cloth tied down or an air-lock in a jar. Unfortunately wine once infected with a vinegar taint cannot be cured, and should be flushed away. The jar needs extra clean washing and sterilisation.

Ropiness

Once in your life time you may see a "ropey" wine. This looks silky and shiny and has a thick appearance. When poured it looks oily. The cause is bacteria of the lactic acid family. The cure is simple. Crush two Campden tablets and beat them into a gallon of wine. The bacteria are connected together in long chains or ropes and the beating breaks them up. Use a long wooden spoon and make a good job of it. Then store in a corked jar for a week or so until the wine looks normal again and a sediment of dead bacteria can be seen on the bottom of the jar. Now rack off the clean wine into a sterilised jar in the usual way. The wine will not be harmed nor the flavour impaired.

Hygiene

Normal standards of usual kitchen hygiene should always be observed. Wash and thoroughly dry every piece of equipment after use and put it away in a dry place. Leave nothing damp because the damp attracts moulds. Any spilt wine on the floor or jar should be wiped clean WITHOUT DELAY. Never leave jars and bottles with traces of wine in them and never use jars or bottles that have traces of

58

wine in them. To do so is to ask for infection. Always drain jars and bottles dry before putting them away and store them in a dry place. Nevertheless, always rinse jars, bottles and all equipment in a sulphite solution before use. The importance of cleanliness cannot be over-emphasised. It is equally important to avoid using any metal equipment other than stainless steel.

Hazes

Most wines quickly fall bright of their own accord after the first racking following the termination of fermentation. If a wine does not do so it should in the first instance be fined. If it is not then clear within say, 2 weeks it should be filtered. The simple and effective kit marketed by Boots will clear most hazy wines quickly and so avoid oxidation. Detailed and easy to follow instructions are supplied with each kit, including line drawings with the name of every part and its function in the filter.

There are however, two hazes which need special treatment caused by pectin and starch. All the recipes in this book include pectin destroying enzyme when necessary, because it is easier to prevent this haze than it is to clear it. It can be identified by placing a few drops of hazy wine in some methylated spirits. If "strings" appear then the wine has a pectin haze and a heavy dose of a pectin destroying enzyme will have to be stirred into the wine which must then be left in a warm place for a few days.

A starch haze can be identified by dropping some wine into iodine. If the yellowy-brown iodine turns blue then the wine contains starch. Use fungal amylase to precipitate the haze.

Sorbate

Some suppliers recommend potassium sorbate for terminating the fermentation of a sweet wine, for stabilising it, as they say. Whilst it does this effectively, it sometimes produces an unpleasant geranium smell in the wine. This is caused by the action of lactic bacilli on the sorbate. 2 crushed Campden tablets are equally effective and produce no side effects.

Cloudy wine falls bright and is racked off its lees into a clean jar

Sherry

One of the most popular wines amongst sophisticated palates is sherry and it is one that is very complicated to make commercially. In the first instance the must is fermented in the presence of air in contradiction to the making of other wines. The fermentation jar is only nine tenths filled and so too is the storage jar. Instead of using an air-lock a plug of cotton wool is used in the neck of the jar. This enables air to enter the jar while the cotton wool acts as a filter of spores and germs.

In the commercial preparation of sherry the wines frequently change their characteristics during maturation and then they are blended together with wines from other years in a solera system that may consist of three or four or thirteen or fourteen tiers. In effect, as wine is drawn out of the bottom cask it is topped up from the next oldest which is in turn topped up by the one before that and so on. Sherry has the great characteristic that it fairly readily absorbs the flavours and qualities of other wines. For example if a quarter of a cask full of sherry wine were to be withdrawn and replaced by a wine of a later year, then the new wine would quickly absorb the flavour and character of the old wine and soon you could not tell that some wine had been withdrawn and a different wine added. This is the secret of the solera system and explains why when you buy a bottle of your favourite sherry it always tastes the same as the last one.

Few amateur winemakers have attempted to set up a solera system for home-made sherry but quite good results can be obtained in the following way.

During storage, oxidation of the wine takes place to produce the nutty taste which is so much enjoyed. One special precaution must be taken however: the wine must be fermented to as high an alcoholic content as possible. With the careful addition of several extra doses of sugar during fermentation it is possible to achieve some 16% of alcohol by volume. With this quantity of alcohol present, the oxidation improves the flavour, whereas oxidation of a low alcohol wine spoils it. Commercial sherry is fortified by a further 2% of alcohol before it is shipped to England. If you wish to fortify your sherry you may do so in accordance with the system mentioned under the next heading.

To make a sherry type wine you must not only use base ingredients that would produce a suitable wine but also ferment the must with a good quality sherry yeast in the presence of air. After racking the wine needs to be stored in not completely filled jars for a while. If blending with similar wines from other years can be managed then it is quite possible to produce wine remarkably similar to sherry. One bottle of Spanish sherry brandy added to five bottles of sherry-type wine and left for 6 months also improves the flavour considerably.

Other fortified wines

There is little point in fortifying wine unless you plan to keep it for many years. The best known fortified wine is of course port wine, which consists of about 20% alcohol. The wine is first started in the usual way but before all the sugar has been converted additional alcohol is added to slow down and eventually stop the fermentation. Such a wine needs considerable maturation both in bulk and in bottle to produce a magnificent full-bodied rich wine of great character and is worth all the effort.

At home it is not difficult to make wine similar to port wine. Suitable base ingredients, such as blackberries, elderberries, bilberries, damsons and the like must be used and a port yeast, of course, must be added. Fermentation must be continued with all care to as high an alcoholic content as possible. When fermentation has nearly finished and enough sugar remains to record a specific gravity of 1.015 to 1.020, the wine is racked off, Vodka is added and the wine is matured for a minimum of two years.

How much alcohol to add is indicated by calculations using a Pearson's square as follows :—

A   **B**

C

D   **E**

In the corner marked B write the alcohol content of your wine at present. In the centre marked C write the alcohol content you wish to obtain. In the corner marked D write the difference between these two figures. In the corner marked A write the alcohol content of the spirit being used in fortification. Finally in the corner marked E write the difference between C and A. The proportion D to E is the proportion of spirit you will need to add to your wine.

For example, assume a wine to have an alcohol content of 14 per cent by volume and the Polish spirit to be 100° proof, that is 57 per cent alcohol by volume (100 per cent pure alcohol is rated as 175° proof, therefore 100 divided by 1.75 equals 57 per cent). Assume also a finished wine of 22 per cent alcohol. Then :—

A equals 57.

B equals 14.

C equals 22.

D equals C − B equals 8

E equals A − C equals 35.

Therefore it is necessary to use 8 parts of Polish spirit to 35 parts of wine to achieve the desired fortification, or about 1 bottle of Polish spirit to $4\frac{1}{2}$ bottles of wine.

Madeira is technically similar. The only difference is the use of the soft brown sugar instead of white and of course a Madeira yeast. These provide the caramelised flavour of Madeira.

a. Plastic stoppers and metal cages for sparkling wine

b. Corks, corkers, foils and viscaps for still wines

Sparkling Wine

This is a most refreshing drink and not too difficult to make. Appropriate wine such as apple, pear or gooseberry is made in the usual way to not more than 12% alcohol, matured for 6 months until it is star-bright and then racked into clean champagne bottles. Top up with some syrup and a little champagne yeast. For 6 bottles dissolve $1\frac{1}{2}$ oz (42.5 grams) sugar in 3 fl oz (85 ml) from an active champagne yeast starter bottle. Add $\frac{3}{4}$ fl oz (21 ml) or about a dessertspoonful to each bottle.

Good quality, really tight fitting, hollow plastic stoppers must now be used. Soften them in hot water, ram home tight and wire on. The bottles should be left in a warm place for a week so that the yeast can ferment the sugar in the syrup and produce some carbon dioxide to cause effervescence when the wine is poured. Real champagne corks are made in three parts and glued together. In 1945 just after the war when these special corks were in very short supply they were said to have cost as much as the wine itself! If you cannot obtain hollow plastic stoppers use the very best corks you can get, otherwise you are wasting your time. The carbon dioxide will slowly escape through the pores of ordinary corks and when the wine is poured out it will be flat and lifeless.

The wine should be stored for 6-12 months so that it can mature and develop a good flavour. If the bottles are stored upside down, the sediment will settle in the hollow stoppers and can subsequently be removed in a process known as disgorging. Keeping the bottle upside down and with your thumb near the stopper, remove the wire with your other hand and ease out the stopper containing the sediment. As you do so, move your thumb over the mouth of the bottle and return it to the upright. Keeping your thumb firmly in place pick up another stopper with your other hand and quickly insert it in the bottle as you move away your thumb. The wire cage should be replaced and the bottle may now be handled without risk of clouding the wine.

If the sediment is not so disgorged, great care should be

taken when pouring not to tilt the bottle backwards and forwards since this will stir up the sediment and give the wine a hazy appearance.

Sparkling wine should always be served chilled and poured into flute shaped glasses rather than saucer shaped glasses. This helps considerably to prolong the liveliness of the wine. The coldness tends to inhibit the release of the bubbles of carbon dioxide gas and the tall glasses show the rising bubbles for longer and concentrates them into a smaller area.

Sweet Table Wine

To make a sweet wine that is not too strong in alcohol, it is necessary to stop the fermentation as soon as the required quantity of alcohol has been formed and while there is still residual sugar in the wine.

It is important to carefully calculate the amount of sugar to use and by frequent hydrometer checks to know the right time to terminate fermentation.

Rack the wine into a clean jar and add two crushed Campden tablets per standard gallon jar — nearly 5 litres. Use 4 tablets for 2 gallons (10 litres), 6 for 3 gallons (15 litres) and so on.

Move the jar to as cool a place as possible and as soon as the wine throws a further sediment rack again and filter it. Although no further Campden tablets may be necessary, it is good practice to add one more.

The purpose is to remove the active yeast cells as well as the dead ones and to inhibit any remaining enzyme action.

These sweet wines are very pleasant when served chilled with the dessert course of a meal or with a sweet biscuit or piece of Victoria sponge or the like.

Wines from Grape Juice Concentrates

Although grape juice concentrate has been available to the home wine maker from before 1960 it is only since 1972 that manufacturers have developed the technique of blending different grape juices to produce concentrates that can be made into excellent wines in their own right. France, Germany and Italy would not at first permit their grape juice to be concentrated and so other sources of supply had to be found. No countries concentrate their very best grape juice and so it has taken some time to develop, often by trial and error, blends of grape juice concentrates that make up into the excellent wines now available. The quality of grape juice varies from season to season and although the addition of concentrate has long been used to improve the vinosity of fruit and other wines, the quality of wine that used to be made from straight concentrate was not high.

Happily the situation has changed dramatically and as a result of the research and effort mentioned, high quality concentrates are now available, so blended as to produce wines of distinctive characteristics. Each manufacturer gives specific instructions on each can for making up the contents to the type of wine indicated. The instructions are of the simplest step-by-step kind, and should be carefully followed.

Do remember to sterilise all equipment and bottles with a sulphite solution. Cleanliness is of paramount importance.

Do use a good yeast and activate it in a starter bottle before adding it to the must.

Do remember to keep your wine well protected from infection by keeping it closely covered at all times and by using an air-lock during fermentation.

Do use new corks thoroughly softened by soaking for 24 hours in a sulphite solution. Label each bottle with the

Making wine from grape juice concentrate.

1. Pour the concentrate into 6 pints (3 litres) water.

2 Add an active yeast.

3 Fit an air-lock and ferment.

4 Check the specific gravity. At S.G. 1.010 add 5 oz. (140 grams) sugar. Repeat the process at S.G. 1.002.

5 Fermentation finished. Add wine finings and Campden tablets.

6 Filter or siphon into bottles, cork and label.
Note : Several wines being made at the same time to provide variety of choice.

name and date of the wine.

Do be patient and allow your wine to mature. Although it may be drinkable in 3 months or so, it will be much better at 6 months and better still when it is a year old.

Do make up a variety of different wines so that you eventually have a range from which to choose the most appropriate for a particular purpose. This will increase your satisfaction considerably compared with just drinking the same wine with every meal.

Do remember that if you stop making wine you will eventually have to stop drinking wine, unless you can afford to buy it at from 5 to 10 times the price. Make some wine each week or fortnight as a regular habit. You may even be able to keep some long enough for it to mature completely!

Method

Open an A 2½ size (1 kg) can of grape juice concentrate and pour the contents into a sterile bin, bucket, bowl, preserving pan or the like. Fill the can with tepid water and gently stir with a wooden or plastic spoon to dissolve any crystals of sugar and to clean the can. About 6 pints (3.5 litres) of water must be added.

Stir the mixture thoroughly and then pour it through a clean funnel into a sterile demijohn or glass jar. Pour in an active yeast and nutrient and fit an air-lock. The bored bung should first be softened by soaking it in warm water and the stem of the air-lock should be pushed in as far as possible. Remove any loose moisture and push the bung and air-lock into the neck of the jar as tight as you can. Remove the cap of the air-lock and pour in a teaspoonful or so of water containing a fraction of a Campden tablet. Replace the cap and set the jar in a warm place beside the boiler, in the airing cupboard or a similar situation.

After 10 days, 5 oz (140 grams) of sugar must be added and 5 days later a similar dose; for dry table wines you now have nothing to do until fermentation is finished, usually in about another two weeks, although much longer is not exceptional. As soon as no more bubbles can be seen rising to the surface of the wine, move the jar to the coolest place you can find – the floor of the larder or the garage for example. Leave it in this position for about a week for the sediment to settle, then siphon the clear wine into a sterile jar, add 1 crushed Campden tablet and top up the jar with a little cold boiled water to the bottom of the neck. Fit a clean soft bung – the rubber ones are excellent but insert them moist. Label the jar with the name of the wine and the date and put it into store for 3 months before bottling.

By this time the wine should be star bright and there should be a thin but firm sediment on the bottom of the jar. If the wine is the least bit hazy, it should be fined and filtered before bottling. Fill the bottles to the bottom of the neck so that there is a space of about $\frac{3}{4}$" (2 cm) between the top of the wine and the bottom of the cork when it is pushed in flush with the top of the neck. Label the bottles with the name and date of the wine and store them on their sides for another 3 months at least. In the absence of a proper wine rack, a bottle carton with its 12 divisions is a good substitute. Return the wine to its cold store and get on making some more wine :— Beaujolais type, Burgundy type, Sherry type, Grape and Gooseberry, Grape and Elderberry and so on.

C.W.E. market a "Connoisseur's Choice" range of about 1.5 kg cans of different concentrates to make 6 bottles of wine. Each can contains half as much more grape juice concentrate than other brands and needs no sugar. The wines are therefore fuller and of superior quality, though necessarily more expensive.

When making fruit wines of a specific type, grape juice concentrate of a similar type may be added and this enhances the quality of the wine type.

The new concentrates have the advantage over fruit wines that they can be made at any time and not only when the fruit is in season.

Maturity

1   Make sure that the wine is adequately mature and ready for drinking. It should cause no prickle on the tongue — a common symptom of an unripe wine. It should be smooth and mellow rather than harsh.

Suitability

2   Consider the circumstances in which it is to be served and ensure that the chosen wine is suitable for the purpose. Dry light wines are suitable for drinking at table. Richer and sweeter wines are for drinking after a meal or by themselves. If your guests are inexperienced wine drinkers they will prefer sweeter rather than drier wines.

Temperature

3   (a) Red wines such as elderberry, blackberry, damson etc. should always be served free from chill. This means at a temperature of between 65° and 70°F (18° and 21°C). The optimum temperature is thought to be 68°F (20°C). This mitigates the harshness of the tannin and softens the wine.

(b) White and Rosé wines on the other hand should be served freshly chilled. That is at 45° to 50°F (8° to 10°C). Lacking tannin the coolness helps the wine to "stand up". When warm it tastes rather flabby.

Decanter

4   Wines benefit from a period of up to an hour in a decanter if they have been bottled for any length of time. This enables any unpleasant gases formed during bottle maturation to escape. In addition a small amount of alcohol oxidises and improves the bouquet. Furthermore the wine looks better in a polished decanter than in a bottle.

Glasses

5   (a) Always use plain clear glasses that have been thoroughly cleaned beforehand. Coloured or decorated glasses should be avoided since they

detract from the beauty of the wine.

(b) Glasses for wine should consist of a broad base, a stout stem and an incurved bowl. The glass should be held by the base between the thumb and the fingers. The stem keeps the bowl elevated and removed from fingers, tray, table etc., so that the wine may be seen the more distinctly. The bowl should be incurved so as to retain the bouquet of the wine rather than allow it to escape too readily.

(c) The glass should be suitable in size for the quantity of wine to be consumed. Examples are illustrated.

(d) Glasses should only be filled half to two-thirds full with wine, this provides room for the bouquet to go on top of the wine, saves spillage and also looks more pleasing to the eye.

(e) Wash glasses in warm water containing a little detergent to dissolve traces of glycerine etc. from the wine and greasy finger prints from the bowl, then rinse the glasses thoroughly in clean cold water and drain them dry. Decanters should be treated in the same way. Discard all chipped and cracked glasses.

6 Few wines taste as well on their own as they do with food. Selecting the right wine for the food and the right food for the wine is something of an art, but it is one well worth studying. In general serve:

Food

(a) Rosé and light wines, both red and white, with light food.

(b) Dry white wines with poultry, pork and fish.

(c) Dry red wines with roast meats, dark hued fish such as mullet and, of course, cheese.

(d) Sweet white wines with the dessert course, sweet biscuits and cake.

(e) Sweet red wines with cheese, nuts and apples after a meal.

(f) Sparkling wines and dry sherry types as aperitifs.

Try to ensure that the wine complements the food and that they both taste better for being together.

7 Wine always tastes better when served in company but the company can influence the wine. To wine lovers you can serve your best wine and know that it will be appreciated and that the occasion will be enhanced. On other people good wine can be wasted and you may be better advised to serve tea, coffee, spirits or beer. Always think of your companions when selecting wines to serve to them. If they enjoy only a small glass of sweet wine then you are wasting your time and reputation in serving them dry wine no matter how good it is. On the other hand if they enjoy dry wines they will not think highly of you for a succession of sweet wines.

8 When you have satisfied yourself that your wine is mature, suitable for the occasion, served at the right temperature, from a decanter into a clear glass, that it accompanies appropriate food and will be enjoyed by the right company, then it is the right time to drink it.

Pick up the half filled glass by the stem, hold it firmly by the base in such a manner that a good light shows through it. Examine the clarity, inspect the hue. Is it starbright, crystal clear, free from the least trace of lees or haze? Is the colour clean and attractive? Do you enjoy looking at it and do you feel justly proud of your endeavour?

If the answer is an undeniable yes – as it should be – then raise the glass to your nose, first for a passing sniff and then for a deep inhalation. Get your nose well into the glass, open your lips ever so slightly and breathe in so that the bouquet wafts into every nerve cell in the nose. The smell should be clean, attractive, vinous, possibly subtly resembling a main ingredient. It should be finely balanced so that you are not unpleasantly aware of any of the component parts such as acid, alcohol, tannin, sugar etc.

So now take a mouthful, swallow the wine slowly as you concentrate your faculties upon the taste, texture and pleasure of it. For a few moments meditate silently. Was it clean, pleasing, well-balanced and in harmony with the bouquet?

This sensation, known as the fairwell, is a pleasure, or otherwise, which develops on the very back of the tongue between 30 and 60 seconds after swallowing the wine. A good wine should be a great joy here. An unbalanced or less than perfect wine will show weakness here.

If you have made your wine well you should have a feeling of deep satisfaction come over you. There is no reason why you should not succeed almost every time if you try hard enough. It is unlikely that you will achieve perfection every time since even the professionals cannot do this. But it is surprising how often you can get very close.

A silver salver shows off wine to perfection

Decanters and glasses ideal for wine Copita for aperitifs, dessert wines and liqueurs. Goblets for red wine. Long stemmed goblet suitable for cold white wine. Flute for sparkling wine. Assorted styles are available through stores like Timothy Whites Ltd.

Recipes

General

All of the following recipes will be found to give good results. They have been developed during 30 years practical experience and in the light of the best theoretical knowledge available. But "one man's meat is another man's poison" and whilst the result of making up these recipes will please most people most of the time, they cannot hope to please all people all of the time. Variations in palate and variations in the quality of the fruit or other ingredients together with variable conditions in the making, and above all in the drinking of them, will inevitably produce the occasional wine which you may not enjoy as much as others. This is simply being honest and applies to the commercial wine maker just as much as to the amateur. That is why the majority of commercial wines that you can buy are a blend of several different wines from different vineyards and sometimes from different years as well.

Grape juice concentrate

In almost every recipe it is recommended that some grape juice concentrate be added. Earlier recipes recommended raisins or sultanas but these are not nearly as suitable for improving the vinosity of a wine as grape juice concentrate. The concentrate is more readily assimilated than the dried fruit. Nevertheless raisins or sultanas may always be used as an alternative to the concentrate if you prefer — $\frac{1}{2}$ lb (225 grams) raisins or sultanas replacing $\frac{1}{2}$ pint (250 grams) concentrate. The concentrate with its natural balance of acid, nutrient, tannin and so forth aids fermentation and gives a vinosity to a wine that is often lacking without it. When the cost is spread over the number of bottles produced it is quite inexpensive in relation to the improvement in quality achieved.

78

It is commonly available in 1 kg cans. One can is sufficient to add into 4 gallons (18 litres) of fruit must. Use a quarter of a can in 1 gallon (4.5 litres). Open the can, stir the contents, cover the can with a double layer of polythene film and fasten down with a strong rubber band or an adhesive tape. Store in the refrigerator or some other cool place until it is next required. It will keep for up to two years in these conditions. 3 kg (sufficient for 12 gallons) and 6 kg (sufficient for 24 gallons) quantities are also available in polythene containers with airtight, screw caps, and are the most economical way to buy this important ingredient.

Essential extras

Similarly with the yeast, nutrient, tannin, citric acid, Campden tablets, and pectin destroying enzyme. These can always be bought more cheaply in bulk and are worth keeping by you. Pectolytic enzyme has been recommended but any other proprietary brand may be used.

Water

The recipes give a guide to the quantity of water that may be required. The precise amount will depend on the juiciness of the fruit and the degree of extraction obtained as well as the actual size of the jar used. The standard glass fermentation jar known as a demijohn, for which these recipes have been designed, holds $8\frac{1}{2}$ pints (4.8 litres). Similar jars may hold a little more or less.

Teaspoon measure

The teaspoon measure frequently mentioned is the 5 ml plastic spoon universally supplied with medicines, or any modern shallow bowled teaspoon.

Sugar

The sugar quantities have been carefully calculated to produce wine of about 12% alcohol from average quality fruit. It is advisable to use a hydrometer to check the specific gravity of the must prior to the addition of the yeast. From this figure can be calculated the precise quantity of sugar that it is necessary to add to produce a wine of a specific alcohol content.

Where several wines are made in exactly the same way, cross reference is made to avoid too much repetition.

A vast number of recipes have been given but the range is really limitless. Variations can be made depending on the ingredients available. Avoid all tuberous flowers, however, which are frequently poisonous, and anything very strongly flavoured such as onion. The results are awful even if they are not actually poisonous.

When using canned fruits always include the juice. Experience has shown that fruits tend to make the best wines and that the right sort of grape more often produces a better wine than other fruits. Whilst this statement can hardly be denied, note all the reservations "fruits TEND to make—" does not *exclude* other ingredients ever making good wines. "The right sort of grape more often produces a better wine" by no means excludes other fruits. Indeed the wrong sort of grape can produce a wine much inferior to wine from other fruits.

These recipes will produce you good, sound wine averaging a comparative worth of £1 a bottle. Sometimes you will be lucky and produce some worth £2.00 or more. They are at least as good as the Continental vin ordinaire and frequently better.

Don't make one wine and wait a year for the result before trying again. Rather make as many different kinds as you can during the first year so that in subsequent years you can make larger quantities of the ones you like best.

Start by making up a few cans of different grape juice concentrates. They mature more quickly than other wines and will give you something to drink whilst waiting for your fruit wines to mature. You will also gain a little experience in the different techniques.

Attractive labels and caps on finished bottles.

The Recipes

1 APPLE (dry)

9 lb mixed cooking
apples   4 kg
½ pint white grape juice
concentrate
                250 grams
1¾ lb white sugar
                800 grams
4½ pints cold water
                2.5 litres

1 tsp. citric acid
½ tsp. tannin
pectic enzyme
Campden tablets
nutrient
Champagne yeast

1   Pour the water into a mashing bin and stir in the acid, tannin, pectic enzyme and 1 crushed Campden tablet.
2   Wash the apples and remove any bad parts. Crush them into a coarse mash and drop them into the bin without delay to avoid browning.
3   Cover the bin and leave in a warm place for 24 hours.
4   Stir in the grape juice concentrate, nutrient and yeast, cover and ferment on the pulp for 7 days, stirring twice daily.
5   Strain and press the fruit till dry, stir in the sugar, pour into a fermentation jar, top up with cold boiled water, fit an air-lock and continue fermentation to the end.
6   Rack into a clean jar, top up, add 1 crushed Campden tablet, bung tight, label and store for 2 months.
7   If wine is not now clear, fine or filter, then store for 6 months, bottle and store for a further 3 months.
8   At the bottling stage this wine may be turned into sparkling wine with excellent results.
9   A few quince, crab apples or the cydonia japonica fruit, mixed in with the apples, improves the bouquet and flavour.

2 APPLE (sweet)

11 lb mixed apples 5 kg
½ pint white grape juice
   concentrate 250 grams

2 lb white sugar
                     900 grams
Sauternes yeast

1   Prepare as previously.
2   Check the S.G. during jar fermentation and when 1.015 is reached remove the jar to a cool place, rack into a clean jar containing 2 crushed Campden tablets to terminate fermentation.
3   Top up, bung tight, label and store in a cold place until a firm deposit is formed
4   Filter into a clean jar to remove all the yeast cells, then store.

3 APPLE (medium sweet)

1 quart apple juice
   concentrate   1 litre
½ pint white grape juice
   concentrate 250 grams
2 lb sugar   900 grams

6 pints water   3.5 litres
1 tsp. citric acid
½ tsp. tannin
nutrient
Champagne yeast

1   Mix all the ingredients together and ferment under an air-lock in a warm place.
2   Rack at S.G. 1.008 and add 2 crushed Campden tablets. Rack again when the wine begins to clear and again when bright.

4 APPLE CIDER

13 lb mixed mellow
  cider apples   6 kg
pectic enzyme
Campden tablets

nutrient
Champagne yeast
(no water)

1   Wash the apples and crush them thoroughly until they become a fine mash.
2   Stir in the pectic enzyme and 2 crushed Campden tablets, cover closely and leave in a warm place for 24 hours.
3   Next day put the mash in a linen cloth or bag and press out all the juice till the pulp is dry.
4   Stir in the nutrient and yeast, pour into a fermentation jar, but leave some headroom in the jar in case of frothing.
5   As soon as fermentation calms down fit an air-lock and ferment to dryness.
6   Alternatively, stop fermentation as S.G. 1.006 by racking and adding another 2 Campden tablets. This produces a slightly sweet cider.

Note: Cider is usually ready for drinking in 4 to 6 months and does not keep well since the alcohol content is only 7% or 8%.

Since no water is required there is no dilution and therefore no acid, tannin or sugar are needed.

5 APPLE, CRAB

5 lb mellow crab apples
  (the creamy red, egg
  shaped John Downey
  variety is excellent) 2.25 kg
½ pint white grape juice
  concentrate 250 grams
1¾ lb approx. sugar 800 grams

4½ pints water 2.25 litres
1 tsp. citric acid
½ tsp. tannin
pectic enzyme
Campden tablets
nutrient
Champagne yeast

1   Prepare and make the wine as for Recipe No. 1, but terminate fermentation at S.G. 1.008 by racking and adding 2 crushed Campden tablets.

84

6 APPLE, DRIED

2 lb dried apple rings
   or slices   900 grams
½ pint white grape juice
   concentrate 250 grams
1¾ lb sugar   800 grams
7 pints water   4 litres

2 tsp. citric acid
½ tsp. tannin
pectic enzyme
Campden tablets
nutrient
Champagne yeast

1   Chop up the apples and put them into a bin containing 6 pints (3.5 litres) of water, the acid, pectic enzyme, tannin and 1 crushed Campden tablet.
2   Cover and leave in a warm place for 24 hours.
3   Stir in the grape juice concentrate, nutrient and yeast and ferment on the pulp for 4 days, then strain and press hard.
4   Dissolve the sugar in a pint (½ litre) of warm water, add it to the must, pour into a fermentation jar, if necessary top up, and ferment to dryness.

7 APPLE & BANANA

Make as for Recipe No. 2 but mash and add 6 freshly peeled very ripe bananas when the apples are crushed.
This makes a sweet wine with greater body.

8 APPLE & BILBERRY

Add to any of the apple recipes 4 oz (100 grams) dried bilberries or 1 lb (450 grams) of canned or bottled bilberries when the apples are crushed. This improves the body and tannin content, and makes a light red wine.

9 APPLE & BLACKBERRY

Add to any of the apple recipes 1 lb (500 grams) of fresh or frozen blackberries when the apples are crushed.
This produces another excellent light red wine.

10 APPLE & ELDERBERRY

Add to any of the apple recipes 4 oz (100 grams) of dried, or 1 lb (450 grams) of fresh elderberries when the apples are crushed.

This is a great favourite and adds to one's stock of red wines, which are often in short supply.

11 APRICOT (dry)

4 lb fresh apricots
    1.80 kg
$\frac{1}{2}$ pint white grape juice
  concentrate 250 grams
2 lb sugar   900 grams
$4\frac{1}{2}$ pints water 2.25 litres

no acid
$\frac{1}{2}$ tsp. tannin
pectic enzyme
Campden tablets
nutrient
Bordeaux yeast

1   Wash the apricots, remove and throw away the stones, cut up or crush the fruit.
2   Pour on $4\frac{1}{2}$ pints (2.25 litres) of hot water and when cool add 1 Campden tablet and the pectic enzyme.
3   Next day stir in the grape juice concentrate and tannin, together with the yeast.
4   Ferment for 4 days, then strain, stir in the sugar, pour into a fermentation jar, top up with cold boiled water if necessary and continue fermentation under an air-lock to dryness.

12 APRICOT (sweet)

5 lb of fresh apricots
    2.25 kg
$\frac{1}{2}$ pint white grape juice
  concentrate 250 grams
$2\frac{1}{2}$ lb sugar   1.10 kg
$4\frac{1}{2}$ pints water
    2.25 litres

no acid
$\frac{1}{2}$ tsp. tannin
pectic enzyme
Campden tablets
nutrient
Sauternes yeast

Make as for Recipe No. 11 but rack at S.G. 1.020 and add 2 crushed Campden tablets to terminate fermentation.

13 APRICOT, DRIED

¾ lb dried apricots 340 grams
½ pint white grape juice concentrate 250 grams
2 lb sugar 900 grams
7 pints water 4 litres

2 tsp. citric acid
½ tsp. tannin
pectic enzyme
Campden tablets
nutrient
Bordeaux yeast

1 Cut up the apricots and soak overnight in 5 pints (3 litres) of water.
2 Next day, simmer the apricots in the same water for 5 minutes and when cool, strain and press lightly.
3 Stir in the pectic enzyme, acid and tannin, cover closely and leave for 24 hours in a warm place.
4 Next day, stir in the sugar, grape juice concentrate, nutrient and yeast. Pour into a fermentation jar, top up with cold boiled water and ferment under an air-lock to S.G. 1.005.
5 Rack and add 2 crushed Campden tablets to terminate fermentation.

14 APRICOT PULP

1 A2½ size can apricot pulp 1 kg can
½ pint white grape juice concentrate 250 grams
2¼ lb sugar 1 kg
4 pints water 2.25 litres

1 tsp. citric acid
½ tsp. tannin
pectic enzyme
Campden tablets
nutrient
Sauternes yeast

1 Empty the can of pulp into a mashing bin, add 4 pints (2.25 litres) water. Stir in 1 Campden tablet and the pectic enzyme. Cover and leave for 24 hours.
2 Next day add the grape juice concentrate, tannin, nutrient and yeast.
3 Ferment for 7 days stirring twice daily, then strain out the pulp.
4 Stir in the sugar, pour into a fermentation jar, top up with cold boiled water and continue fermentation

under an air-lock to S.G. 1.015.

5   Rack and add 2 Campden tablets to terminate fermentation.

15 APRICOT CONCENTRATE (sweet)

12 oz apricot 350 grams
4½ oz grape juice
   concentrate 125 grams
2¼ lb sugar   1 kg
6 pints water   3.5 litres

2 tsp. citric acid
pectic enzyme
Campden tablets
nutrient
Sauternes yeast

1   Dissolve apricot and grape juice concentrate in 4 pints (2.5 litres) water, stir in 1 Campden tablet, the pectic enzyme and the acid.
2   Cover and leave 24 hours then stir in the sugar, tannin, nutrient and yeast.
3   Ferment in jar for 7 days then stir in the rest of the sugar dissolved in 2 pints (1 litre) of water, and if necessary top up the jar with cold boiled water.
4   Continue fermentation to S.G. 1.020 then rack and add 2 crushed Campden tablets to terminate fermentation.

16 ARTICHOKE

4½ lb artichokes   2 kg
½ pint grape juice
   concentrate 250 grams
2¼ lb sugar   1 kg.
1 oz root ginger 25 grams

4 small lemons
6 pints water   3.5 litres
½ tsp. tannin
nutrient
G.P. yeast

1   Mince the artichokes, thinly pare the lemons, bruise the ginger, add to 4 pints (2.5 litres) water and gently boil for 30 minutes.
2   Strain, stir in the sugar and when cool stir in the grape juice concentrate, the lemon juice, tannin, nutrient and yeast.
3   Pour into a fermentation jar, top up with cold boiled water and ferment under an air-lock to dryness.

Some vegetables suitable for wine making
Beetroot, carrots, parsnips, broad beans, celery, parsley all make good wine.

17 BANANA
(sweet)

4½ lb peeled, very ripe
  bananas   2 kg
2 large lemons
½ pint white grape juice
  concentrate 250 grams
2½ lb sugar   1 kg

7 pints water   4 litres
1 tsp. citric acid
½ tsp. tannin
Campden tablets
nutrient
Cereal yeast

1   Peel the bananas and place them in a muslin bag together with the thinly pared rind of the lemons. Boil them in 5 pints (3 litres) of water for 30 minutes.
2   Strain on to the sugar and stir until it is dissolved.
3   When cool stir in the grape juice concentrate, the lemon juice, acid, tannin, nutrient and an active yeast.
4   Pour into a fermentation jar, top up with cold boiled water, fit an air-lock and ferment to S.G. 1.015.
5   Rack and add 2 crushed Campden tablets to terminate fermentation.

18 BANANA, DRIED

12 oz dried bananas
          350 grams
2 large lemons
½ pint white grape juice
  concentrate 250 grams
2¼ lb sugar   1 kg

7 pints water   4 litres
1 tsp. citric acid
½ tsp. tannin
Campden tablets
nutrient
Cereal yeast

1   Soak the bananas overnight in about 4 pints (2 litres) of cold water then proceed as for Recipe No. 17.

19 BANANA & ROSEHIP

12 oz dried bananas
350 grams
3½ oz dried rosehip
shells   100 grams
½ pint grape juice
concentrate 250 grams

2¼ lb sugar   1 kg
7 pints water   4 litres
½ oz citric acid 15 grams
½ tsp. tannin
Campden tablets
nutrient
Sherry yeast

1   Soak the bananas and rosehip shells overnight in 4 pints (2 litres) of cold water.
2   Proceed as for Recipe No. 17.

20 BEETROOT

4½ lb beetroot   2 kg
½ pint red grape juice
concentrate 250 grams
2¾ lb demerara sugar
1.25 kg
6 pints water   3.5 litres
¾ oz citric acid 20 grams

½ oz whole ginger
10 grams
6 cloves
½ tsp. tannin
nutrient
Madeira yeast

(If demerara sugar is not available use white sugar and a Port yeast).
1   Scrub the beet thoroughly to remove every trace of earth.
2   Dice the beet and boil till cooked in half the water together with the spices.
3   Strain on to 2 lb (1 kg) sugar and stir till dissolved, then leave to cool.
4   Stir in the grape juice concentrate, acid and tannin together with the nutrient and an active yeast.
5   Top up to the shoulder only of the jar, fit an air-lock and ferment for 14 days.
6   Take out some wine, dissolve the rest of the sugar in it and return it to the jar, replace the air-lock and continue fermentation.
7   This wine will finish strong and sweet and needs long storage before it is at its best.

21 BILBERRY I

1 A2½ size can or jar of
   bilberries   1 kg
½ pint red grape juice
   concentrate 250 grams
2 lb sugar   900 grams
5 pints water   3 litres

2 tsp. citric acid
pectic enzyme
Campden tablets
nutrient
Burgundy yeast

1 Empty the contents of the can or jar into a mashing bin and pour on 5 pints (3 litres) boiling water.

2 When cool add all the other ingredients except the sugar, stir well, then check the specific gravity. The difference between this figure and 1.090 indicates the amount of sugar to add later. The bilberries will be in a syrup for which it is impossible to make a precise allowance.

3 Ferment on the pulp for 5 days, stirring twice daily, then strain and press. Stir in the required amount of sugar, pour into a fermentation jar, top up with cold boiled water, fit an air-lock and continue fermentation to dryness.

This makes an excellent table wine well worth making in larger quantities.

22 BILBERRY II

9 oz dried bilberries
              250 grams
½ pint red grape juice
   concentrate 250 grams
2 lb sugar   900 grams

7 pints water   4 litres
2 tsp. citric acid
pectic enzyme
nutrient
Burgundy yeast

1 Pour 5 pints (3 litres) of boiling water over the bilberries and when cool crush them and add the pectic enzyme and acid. Leave over night.

2 Next day stir in the grape juice concentrate, nutrient and yeast.

3 Ferment on the pulp for 5 days then strain, stir in the sugar, pour into a fermentation jar, top up with cold boiled water and continue fermentation under an air-lock to dryness.

23 BLACKBERRY (dry)

3½ lb fresh picked garden blackberries 1.5 kg
½ pint red grape juice concentrate 250 grams
2 lb sugar 900 grams

6 pints water 3.5 litres
1 tsp. citric acid
½ tsp. tannin
pectic enzyme
nutrient
Burgundy yeast

1 Wash, drain and crush the blackberries, pour on 6 pints (3.5 litres) of boiling water, and when cool add the acid, tannin and pectic enzyme, the red grape juice concentrate, nutrient and yeast.

2 Ferment for 5 days, then strain and press, stir in the sugar, pour into a fermentation jar, top up with cold boiled water and continue fermentation to dryness.

24 BLACKBERRY (sweet)

4½ lb fresh picked hedgerow blackberries 2 kg
½ pint red grape juice concentrate 250 grams
2 lb sugar 900 grams
6 pints water 3.5 litres

1 tsp. citric acid
½ tsp. tannin
pectic enzyme
Campden tablets
nutrient
Port yeast

1 Prepare as in Recipe No. 23 but add 1 lb (500 grams) sugar after straining and the remainder in 3 equal doses at 8 day intervals.

2 Finish this strong wine sweet at about S.G. 1.020 and mature it for at least 18 months.

25 BLACKBERRY, CANNED

1 A2½ size can blackberries 1 kg
½ pint red grape juice concentrate 250 grams
2 lb sugar 900 grams
5 pints water 3 litres

1 tsp. citric acid
½ tsp. tannin
pectic enzyme
Campden tablets
nutrient
Burgundy yeast

Make in the same way as Recipe No. 21.

26 BLACKBERRY & APPLE PURÉE

1 A2½ size can blackberry and apple purée or pie filling 1 kg
½ pint red grape juice concentrate 250 grams
2 lb sugar 900 grams
6 pints water 3.5 litres

1 tsp. citric acid
½ tsp. tannin
pectic enzyme
Campden tablets
nutrient
Bordeaux yeast

1　Pour 5 pints (3 litres) boiling water over the purée in a mashing bin and when cool stir in the acid, tannin, pectic enzyme, red grape juice concentrate, nutrient and yeast.

2　Ferment for 5 days, stirring twice daily.

3　Strain, stir in the sugar, pour into a fermentation jar, top up, fit an air-lock and ferment to dryness.

27 BLACKCURRANT I (sweet)

2¼ lb ripe blackcurrants when washed and stripped from their stalks 1 kg
½ pint red grape juice concentrate 250 grams
2¾ lb sugar 1.25 kg

6 pints water 3.5 litres
½ tsp. tannin
pectic enzyme
Campden tablets
nutrient
Port yeast

1　Pour 5 pints (3 litres) boiling water over the fruit in a mashing bin and when cool stir in the pectic enzyme, tannin, grape juice concentrate, nutrient and yeast.

2　Ferment for 5 days, stirring twice daily.

3　Strain out the fruit, stir in 1 lb (500 grams) sugar, pour into a fermentation jar and leave room for the rest of the sugar.

4　Fit an air-lock and ferment for 8 days.

5　Stir in the remaining sugar in 3 equal doses at 8 day intervals.

6　Finish this strong wine sweet at about S.G. 1.020.

Because of its high acidity this fruit does not make a good dry wine by itself.

28
BLACKCURRANT
II

26 fl oz (standard bottle) blackcurrant syrup   750 ml
1 pint red grape juice concentrate 500 grams
4½ lb sugar   2 kg

12 pints water   7 litres
1 tsp. citric acid
1 tsp. tannin
Campden tablets
nutrient
Port yeast

The quantities shown here will make 12 bottles of wine.

1   Stir all the ingredients together in a 2 gallon (9 litres) bin and ferment in a warm place to S.G. 1.015.
2   Rack and add 4 crushed Campden tablets to terminate fermentation.
3   Store for 6 months then siphon into 12 bottles.
This is a fast maturing wine well worth making.

29
BLACKCURRANT
III

1 A2½ size can blackcurrants   1 kg
½ pint red grape juice concentrate 250 grams
2¼ lb sugar   1 kg
4 pints water   2.25 litres

½ tsp. citric acid
½ tsp. tannin
pectic enzyme
nutrient
Port yeast

1   Open the can, pour the contents in a mashing bin, crush the blackcurrants, add the water, acid, tannin, pectic enzyme, grape juice concentrate, nutrient and yeast.
2   Ferment on the pulp for 5 days, stirring twice daily.
3   Strain out the fruit, stir in the sugar, pour into a fermentation jar, top up with cold boiled water, fit an air-lock and continue fermentation to S.G. 1.015.
4   Rack and add 2 crushed Campden tablets to terminate fermentation, then store for 6 months before bottling.

30 BRAMBLE TIPS (dry)

4½ lb young blackberry shoots   2 kg
½ pint white grape juice concentrate 250 grams
1¾ lb sugar   800 grams

7 pints water   4 litres
2 tsp. citric acid
½ tsp. tannin
nutrient
Bordeaux yeast

1   Wash the shoots, chop them up and boil them in 4 pints (2 litres) water for 30 minutes.
2   Strain and stir in the sugar, grape juice concentrate, acid and tannin, till all is dissolved.
3   When cool, add the nutrient and yeast, pour into a fermentation jar, top up with cold boiled water, fit an air-lock and ferment to dryness.

31 BRAMBLE TIPS (sweet)

5 lb young blackberry shoots   2.25 kg
½ pint white grape juice concentrate 250 grams
2¼ lb sugar   1 kg
7 pints water   4 litres

2 tsp. citric acid
½ tsp. tannin
Campden tablets
nutrient
Sauternes yeast

Make as Recipe No. 30 but terminate fermentation at S.G. 1.015.

32 BROAD BEAN (dry)

4½ lb shelled broad beans at end of season   2 kg
½ pint white grape juice concentrate 250 grams
1¾ lb sugar   800 grams

7 pints water   4 litres
2 tsp. citric acid
½ tsp. tannin
nutrient
Hock yeast

1   Boil the beans in 4 pints (2 litres) water for 1 hour, then continue as for Recipe No. 30.

33 BULLACE
(sweet)

3 lb bullaces   1.5 kg
$\frac{1}{2}$ pint red grape juice
   concentrate 250 grams
$2\frac{1}{2}$ lb sugar   1.1 kg
6 pints water   3.5 litres
1 tsp. citric acid

$\frac{1}{2}$ tsp. tannin
pectic enzyme
Campden tablets
nutrient
Sauternes yeast

1   Wash and stalk the bullaces, place them in a mashing bin and pour on 5 pints (3 litres) boiling water.
2   When cool mash the fruit with your hands and remove the stones.
3   Add the citric acid, tannin, pectic enzyme and 1 Campden tablet.
4   Next day stir in the grape juice concentrate, nutrient and yeast and ferment on the pulp for 5 days, stirring twice daily.
5   Strain out the fruit, stir in the sugar, pour into a fermentation jar, top up, fit an air-lock and continue fermentation to S.G. 1.015.
6   Rack and add 2 crushed Campden tablets to terminate fermentation.

34 CARROT
(sweet)

$4\frac{1}{2}$ lb good quality
   mid-season carrots 2 kg
$\frac{1}{2}$ pint white grape juice
   concentrate 250 grams
$2\frac{1}{2}$ lb sugar   1.1 kg
7 pints water   4 litres

$\frac{3}{4}$ oz citric acid 20 grams
$\frac{1}{2}$ tsp. tannin
Campden tablets
nutrient
G.P. yeast

1   Top and tail the carrots and scrub them clean and free from every trace of earth.
2   Chop them into small dice and boil them for 20 minutes in 4 pints (2 litres) water.
3   Strain on to half the sugar, grape juice concentrate, citric acid and tannin, and stir till all is dissolved.
4   When cool add the nutrient and yeast, pour into a fermentation jar, top up with water but leave space

for the rest of the sugar.

5   Fit an air-lock and ferment for 8 days.
6   Add the rest of the sugar in 3 equal doses at 8 day intervals and finish the wine sweet at S.G. 1.020.

35 CELERY

4½ lb celery   2 kg
½ pint white grape juice
   concentrate 250 grams
31 oz sugar   850 grams

7 pints water   4 litres
2 tsp. citric acid
¼ tsp. tannin
Hock yeast

1   Cut off the leaves, stalk and any damaged parts, then scrub the celery spotlessly clean.
2   Chop into small pieces and boil till tender in 4 pints (2 litres) of water.
3   Strain on to the sugar, grape juice concentrate, acid and tannin, and stir till all is dissolved.
4   When cool pour into a fermentation jar, add the nutrient and yeast, top up with cold boiled water, fit an air-lock and ferment to dryness.

36 CHERRY "BRANDY"

2¼ lb morello cherries —
   fresh, frozen, canned
   or bottled   1 kg
4 bottles home brewed
   ale, or
3 bottles wine made
   from red grape juice
   concentrate

18 oz sugar   500 grams
1 tsp. tartaric acid, or
   2 tsp. if using ale
½ tsp. tannin
nutrient
Port yeast — very active

1   Dissolve half the sugar in the ale or wine and pour on to the cherries from which you have previously removed the pips.
2   Add the acid, tannin, nutrient and well activated yeast.
3   Ferment in a warm place, stirring daily and adding extra sugar from time to time to keep the S.G. around 1.020.

4   Continue fermentation as long as possible, then strain out the cherries which are delicious in a trifle or tart. Rack the wine into bottles and mature for 1 year. Superb.

37 CHERRY (dry)

4½ lb mixed cherries, eating and cooking varieties 2 kg	1 tsp. citric acid
½ pint red grape juice concentrate 250 grams	½ tsp. tannin
1¾ lb sugar 800 grams	pectic enzyme
6 pints water 3.5 litres	Campden tablets
	nutrient
	Bordeaux yeast

1   Wash and stalk the cherries and place them in a mashing bin.
2   Pour on 5 pints (3 litres) boiling water and when cool mash them with your hands, removing all the stones.
3   Add the acid, tannin, pectic enzyme and 1 crushed Campden tablet, cover and leave for 24 hours.
4   Add the grape juice concentrate, nutrient and yeast and ferment on the pulp for 5 days, stirring twice daily.
5   Strain out the fruit, stir in the sugar, pour into a fermentation jar, top up with cold boiled water, fit an air-lock and continue fermentation to dryness.

38 CHERRY
(sweet)

4½ lb mixed cherries and
  ½ lb morello cherries
                    2.25 kg
½ pint red grape juice
  concentrate 250 grams
2¾ lb sugar   1.25 kg
6 pints water   3.5 litres

1 tsp. citric acid
½ tsp. tannin
pectic enzyme
Campden tablets
nutrient
Port yeast

1   Prepare as for Recipe No. 37 but include only half the
     sugar at first. Add the remainder in 3 equal doses at
     8 day intervals.
2   Finish this strong wine sweet at about S.G. 1.020.

39 CHERRY
(medium sweet)

1 A2½ size can of
  cherries   1 kg
½ pint red grape juice
  concentrate 250 grams
2¼ lb sugar   1 kg
5 pints water   3 litres

1 tsp. citric acid
½ tsp. tannin
Campden tablets
nutrient
Port yeast

1   Place the contents of the can into a mashing bin and
     remove the stones.
2   Dissolve the acid, tannin and grape juice concentrate
     in warm water and pour it over the cherries.
3   Add the nutrient and yeast and ferment for 5 days,
     stirring twice daily.
4   Strain out the fruit, stir in the sugar, pour into a
     fermentation jar, top up, fit an air-lock and ferment to
     S.G. 1.010.
5   Rack into a clean jar and add 2 crushed Campden
     tablets to terminate fermentation.

Ideal bottle racks

40 CHERRY PLUM

4½ lb cherry plums 2 kg
½ pint grape juice
  concentrate (red or
  white)   250 grams
2¼ lb sugar   1 kg
6 pints water   3.5 litres

2 tsp. citric acid
½ tsp. tannin
pectic enzyme
Campden tablets
nutrient
Sauternes yeast

1   Stalk and wash the fruit, split them in half and discard the stones.
2   Pour 5 pints (3 litres) boiling water over the fruit and when cool stir in the acid, tannin, pectic enzyme and 1 Campden tablet.
3   Next day stir in the grape juice concentrate, nutrient and yeast, and ferment for 5 days stirring twice daily.
4   Strain out the fruit, stir in the sugar, pour into a fermentation jar, top up, fit an air-lock and ferment to S.G. 1.010.
5   Rack into a clean jar and add 2 crushed Campden tablets.

41 COFFEE

9 oz bottle coffee
  essence   250 grams
1 pint white grape juice
  concentrate 500 grams
2lb brown sugar
              900 grams

7 pints water   4 litres
2 tsp. citric acid
½ tsp. tannin
Campden tablets
nutrient
Madeira yeast

1   Stir all the ingredients into 5 pints (3 litres) of tepid water, pour into a fermentation jar, top up, fit an air-lock and ferment to S.G. 1.015.
2   Rack into a clean jar and add 2 crushed Campden tablets to terminate fermentation.
    This is an unusual but very pleasant wine with a coffee bouquet and flavour.

42 COLTSFOOT

1¾ pints fresh coltsfoot
flowers cleaned for use
1 litre
or 1 small packet of dried
flowers from a
herbalist
1 pint white grape juice
concentrate
500 grams

1¾ lb white sugar
800 grams
6 pints water   *3.5 litres*
2 tsp. citric acid
½ tsp. tannin
Campden tablets
nutrient
Sauternes yeast

1   Pour 4 pints *(2 litres)* hot water on to the petals and macerate them with a wooden or plastic spoon.
2   When cool stir in the acid, tannin and 1 crushed Campden tablet, cover and leave in a warm place.
3   Macerate the petals daily for 4 days.
4   Dissolve the grape juice concentrate and sugar in 1 quart *(1 litre)* of warm water and strain the flower water into the syrup.
5   Stir in the nutrient and yeast, pour into a fermentation jar, top up with cold boiled water, fit an air-lock and ferment to S.G. 1.015.
6   Rack into a clean jar and add 2 crushed Campden tablets to terminate fermentation.

Note: The sweet bouquet of all flower wines needs to be followed by a sweet wine. In the author's opinion flower wines do not make attractive dry wines. All flower wines are best made in the manner described above.

43 COWSLIP 1¾ pints of flowers
picked free from all
green   1 litre

Other ingredients and method as for Recipe No. 42.

44 CURRANT (dry) 2¾ lb best quality dried
currants   1.25 kg
9 oz white sugar
                250 grams
7 pints water   4 litres

2 tsp. citric acid
½ tsp. tannin
Campden tablets
nutrient
Hock yeast

Method as for Recipe No. 128.

45 DAMSON (dry) 3¼ lb damsons   1.5 kg
½ pint red grape juice
concentrate 250 grams
1¾ lb sugar   800 grams
6 pints water   3.5 litres
2 tsp. citric acid

½ tsp. tannin
pectic enzyme
Campden tablets
nutrient
Burgundy yeast

1 Stalk the damsons and wash them in hot water to dissolve the waxy bloom which causes a haze in the wine. Rinse them in clean hot water and then place them in a mashing bin.
2 Pour on 5 pints (3 litres) of hot water, cover and leave to cool.
3 When cool, mash the fruit and remove the stones.
4 Add the acid, tannin, pectic enzyme and 1 crushed Campden tablet. Cover and leave for 24 hours.
5 Stir in the grape juice concentrate, nutrient and yeast and ferment on the pulp for 5 days, stirring twice daily.
6 Strain out the fruit, stir in the sugar, pour into a fermentation jar, top up with water, fit an air-lock and

ferment to dryness.

7 Rack into a clean jar, stir in some fining and leave in a cool place for 7 days. Filter and store for 9 months before siphoning into bottles.

Keep this splendid wine at least another 3 months.

46 DAMSON (sweet)

4½ lb damsons	2 kg	½ tsp. tannin
½ pint red grape juice		pectic enzyme
concentrate	250 grams	Campden tablets
2¾ lb sugar	1.25 kg	nutrient
6 pints water	3.5 litres	Port yeast
2 tsp. citric acid		

Make as for a dry wine – Recipe No. 45 – but add only 1 lb (500 grams) of sugar at first and the remainder in 3 equal doses at 8 day intervals. Finish the wine sweet at about S.G. 1.020 and try to keep it for 2 years before drinking it.

47 DAMSON CREAM

Use 2 lb (1 kg) stoned damsons instead of morello cherries and make as for Recipe No. 36. This is another superb dessert wine.

48 DANDELION

1 quart (1 litre) of dandelion petals picked free from all green.

Other ingredients and method as for Recipe No. 42.

49 DATE

4½ lb stoneless dates 2 kg
½ pint white grape juice
  concentrate 250 grams
1 lb brown sugar
       500 grams

7 pints water   4 litres
¾ oz citric acid 20 grams
½ tsp. tannin
nutrient
Sherry yeast

1 Chop up the dates and gently boil them for ½ hour in 5 pints (3 litres) of water.
2 Strain and when cool stir in the grape juice concentrate, acid, tannin, nutrient and yeast.
3 Pour into a fermentation jar, top up to just below the shoulder and ferment for 10 days under a plug of cotton wool.
4 Stir in the sugar in 2 equal doses at 8 day intervals.
5 Ferment this wine to the highest alcohol content possible and finish it sweet at S.G. 1.020.
6 Rack and store in a jar not quite full under a good plug of cotton wool for 9 months, then bottle and keep for 6 months.

50 ELDERBERRY (dry)

2¼ lb fresh
  elderberries   1 kg
½ pint red grape juice
  concentrate
       250 grams

2 lb sugar   900 grams
7 pints water   4 litres
2 tsp. citric acid
nutrient
Burgundy yeast

1 Remove the berries from every piece of stalk for this imparts a bitter taste to the wine. Rinse them in cold water.
2 Place the berries in a pan with 5 pints (3 litres) of water and simmer them gently for 20 minutes, then strain out the berries, cover the liquor and leave till cool.
3 Stir in the grape juice concentrate, sugar, acid, nutrient and yeast.
4 Pour into a fermentation jar, top up, fit an air-lock and ferment to dryness.
Note : No tannin nor pectic enzyme is required.

106

51 ELDERBERRY
(sweet)

2¼ lb fresh
  elderberries   1 kg
½ pint red grape juice
  concentrate
          250 grams

2¾ lb sugar   1.25 kg
7 pints water   4 litres
2 tsp. citric acid
nutrient
Port yeast

Make as for Recipe No. 50 but add only 1 lb (500 grams) sugar at first and the remainder in three equal doses at 8 day intervals. Mature for at least 1 year.

52 ELDERBERRY & BLACKBERRY

1 lb fresh
1 lb fresh elederberries
          500 grams
2¼ lb blackberries   1 kg

Other ingredients and method as for Recipe No. 50.

53 ELDERBERRY, BLACKBERRY & BLACKCURRANT
(sweet)

1 lb elderberries
          500 grams
2¼ lb blackberries   1 kg
1 lb blackcurrants
          500 grams

½ pint red grape juice
  concentrate
          250 grams
2¾ lb sugar   1.25 kg
6 pints water   3.5 litres
nutrient
Port yeast

Make as for Recipe No. 50 but add only 1 lb (500 grams) sugar at first and the remainder in three equal doses at 8 day intervals. Mature for at least 1 year. No acid is needed.

54 ELDERBERRY & BILBERRY (dry)

1 lb fresh elderberries
  500 grams
1 15½ oz can or bottle
  bilberries   450 grams
1 lb 10 oz sugar
  750 grams

½ pint red grape juice
  concentrate
  250 grams
6 pints water   3.5 litres
2 tsp. citric acid
nutrient
Burgundy yeast

1   Remove the berries from their stalk and simmer them in 5 pints (3 litres) water for 20 minutes. Strain and leave the liquor to cool.
2   Empty the bilberries and their syrup into a mashing bin, add the elderberry liquor, the grape juice concentrate, nutrient and yeast.
3   Ferment on the pulp for 5 days, stirring twice daily.
4   Strain and press the bilberries, stir in the sugar, pour into a fermentation jar, top up, fit an air-lock and ferment to dryness. Many people prefer this wine to a straight elderberry.

55 ELDERBERRY & BILBERRY (sweet)

2¼ lb fresh elderberries
  1 kg
1 15½ oz can or bottle
  of bilberries
  450 grams

2¼ lb sugar   1 kg

Other ingredients and method as for Recipe No. 54 but add only half the sugar at first and the rest in 3 doses at 8 day intervals. Finish this strong sweet wine at S.G. 1.020.
Note: If fresh bilberries are available they should be included with the elderberries and simmered.

108

56 ELDERBERRY & BILBERRY DRIED

4 oz dried elderberries 125 grams
4 oz dried bilberries 125 grams
½ pint red grape juice concentrate 250 grams

2 lb sugar 900 grams
7 pints water 4 litres
2 tsp. citric acid
Campden tablets
nutrient
Burgundy yeast

1 Thoroughly wash the fruit in tepid water containing 1 crushed Campden tablet and a few grains of citric acid. Strain and rinse in clean water.
2 Place the fruit in a pan of hot water and simmer gently for 20 minutes.
3 Continue as in Recipe No. 50.

57 ELDERBERRY, DRIED (dry)

9 oz dried elderberries 250 grams
½ pint red grape juice concentrate 250 grams
2 lb sugar 900 grams

7 pints water 4 litres
2 tsp. citric acid
Campden tablets
nutrient
Burgundy yeast

Make as for Recipe No. 56.

58 ELDERBERRY, DRIED (sweet)

9 oz dried elderberries 250 grams
1 pint red grape juice concentrate 500 grams

2 lb sugar 900 grams
7 pints water 4 litres
2 tsp. citric acid
Campden tablets
Port yeast

1 Make as for Recipe No. 56 but add only half the sugar at first and the remainder in 2 equal doses at 8 day intervals.
2 When S.G. 1.020 is reached after all the sugar has been added, rack into a clean jar and add 2 Campden tablets.

59 ELDERBERRY, DAMSON & APPLE (sweet)

1 lb fresh elderberries
      500 grams
2¼ lb fresh damsons 1 kg
3½ lb cooking apples or
   windfalls   1.5 kg
½ pint red grape juice
   concentrate 250 grams

2¼ lb sugar   1 kg
6 pints water 3.5 litres
1 tsp. citric acid
pectic enzyme
Campden tablets
nutrient
Port yeast

1   Wash and stalk the elderberries, wash and stone the damsons, wash and crush the apples.
2   Drop them as ready into a mashing bin containing 5 pints (3 litres) water, the acid, pectic enzyme, and 1 crushed Campden tablet. Cover and leave overnight.
3   Stir in the grape juice concentrate and half the sugar, the nutrient and the yeast. Ferment on the pulp for 7 days, stirring twice daily.
4   Strain and press the fruit, stir in the rest of the sugar. Pour into a fermentation jar, top up, fit an air-lock and ferment to S.G. 1.020.
5   Rack into a clean jar, add 2 crushed Campden tablets and wine finings. 2 weeks later filter, then mature for 1 year.

60 ELDERBERRY PUNCH

1 bottle elderberry wine
1 small lemon
6 whole cloves
1 large piece root ginger

1 dessertspoonful of
   honey
3 or 4 tablespoonsful
   sugar

1   Pour the wine into a saucepan.
2   Thinly peel the lemon and add the yellow rind to the wine.
3   Well bruise the root ginger and add to the wine with the cloves.
4   Place the saucepan on a slow heat, add the sugar and

honey and stir gently till they are dissolved.

5   Check the temperature of the punch with a culinary thermometer.

6   When the temperature reaches 140°F (60°C) pour the punch into pre-heated glasses and serve with hot mince pies.

Note : The wine may be diluted with not more than a small cup of water (blackcurrant cordial suitably diluted is an alternative). A miniature bottle of rum may be added to make the punch stronger. Make sure that the temperature does not exceed 140°F (60°C) or the alcohol will evaporate.

This really is a superb drink on a cold night. Try it at bedtime or as a welcome to guests.

61 ELDERBERRY & BANANA

Add 1 lb (500 grams) of peeled and very ripe bananas to Recipes 50, 51, 52, 53, 54 and 55 to give extra body to the wine. Similarly ½ lb (125 grams) dried bananas may be added to Recipes 56 and 57.   The flavour is only subtly affected but the fullness is considerably improved.

62 ELDERBERRY & RUNNER BEAN

If you have any runner beans left when the elderberries are ripe, add 1 lb (500 grams) washed, stringed and sliced runner beans to Recipes No. 50 and 51. Alternatively, frozen beans may be used. The wine is given extra body and smoothness.

63 ELDERFLOWER

1 quart (1 litre) elderflowers picked on a dry, sunny day and quite free from leaf stalk and green.

Other ingredients and method as for Recipe No. 42.

64 FIG (dry)

8 oz best dried figs
  225 grams
1 pint white grape juice
  concentrate 500 grams
1¼ lb sugar   600 grams

6 pints water   3.5 litres
6 pints water   3.5 litres
2 tsp. citric acid
½ tsp. tannin
nutrient
G.P. yeast

1   Break the figs in pieces and soak them in 4 pints (2 litres) water overnight.
2   Next day boil them gently in the same water for 10 minutes. As the liquor only is needed for the wine, remove the boiled figs, which can be eaten as a dessert if liked.
3   Dissolve the sugar, acid and tannin in 2 pints (1 litre) of water and mix the two liquids.
4   When cool stir in the grape juice concentrate, add the nutrient and yeast, pour into a fermentation jar, top up, fit an air-lock and ferment to dryness.
Note: Fig has a very powerful flavour and is not attractive if used in greater quantities.

Ingredients for a hot wine punch. Red wine, sugar, lemon, ginger, cloves and honey. N.B. Use the thermometer to check when the temperature reaches 140°F (60°C)

65 FIG (sweet)

9 oz best dried figs
     250 grams
1 pint white grape juice
  concentrate 500 grams
2¼ lb sugar   1 kg

6 pints water   3.5 litres
2 tsp. citric acid
½ tsp. tannin
nutrient
Sauternes yeast

1   Make as for Recipe No. 64 but use only half the sugar at first and the rest in 2 equal doses at 8 day intervals.
2   Rack when S.G. 1.020 is reached after all the sugar has been used, and add 2 crushed Campden tablets.

66 FIG, APRICOT & BANANA (sweet)

7 oz dried figs
     200 grams
7 oz dried apricots
     200 grams
7 oz dried bananas
     200 grams
½ pint white grape juice
  concentrate 250 grams

2¼ lb white sugar   1 kg
7 pints water   4 litres
2 tsp. citric acid
½ tsp. tannin
pectic enzyme
Campden tablets
nutrient
Sauternes yeast

1   Break up the dried fruit and soak it in 4 pints (2 litres) of cold water overnight, together with the acid and pectic enzyme.
2   Next day gently boil the fruit in the same water for about 10 minutes. Remove the boiled fruit and use only the liquor for the wine.
3   Dissolve the sugar, grape juice concentrate and tannin in another 2 pints (1 litre) of water.
4   Mix the 2 liquids together, add the nutrient and yeast, pour into a fermentation jar, top up, fit an air-lock and ferment to S.G. 1.020.
5   Terminate fermentation by racking and adding 2 crushed Campden tablets.

67 GERANIUM LEAF
(Pelargonium quercifolium)

1 quart (1 litre) of leaves, freshly washed from dust and dirt.

Other ingredients and method as for Recipe No. 42.

Note: Do not use any other geranium or pelargonium leaves since they are not suitable for wine-making.

68 GINGER WINE

2 oz root ginger 60 grams
1 pint red grape juice
  concentrate 500 grams
$2\frac{1}{4}$ lb sugar   1 kg
6 pints water   3.5 litres

$\frac{1}{2}$ oz citric acid 15 grams
$\frac{1}{2}$ tsp. tannin
Campden tablets
nutrient
Tokay yeast

1   Place the ginger in a cotton bag and bruise it thoroughly.

2   Boil the ginger, half the sugar and all the acid in about 5 pints (3 litres) of water for 20 minutes.

3   Remove the bag of ginger, squeezing out all the syrup with a wooden spoon.

4   When cool stir in the grape juice concentrate, tannin, nutrient and an active yeast.

5   Pour into a fermentation jar and top up to the lower part of the shoulder. Fit an air-lock and ferment for 10 days.

6   Stir in the rest of the sugar, top up the jar and continue fermentation to S.G. 1.020.

7   Rack into a clean jar containing 2 crushed Campden tablets to terminate fermentation.

69 GOOSEBERRY (dry)

3 lb 5 oz green gooseberries, nearly ripe but still hard 1.5 kg
½ pint white grape juice concentrate 250 grams
2 lb white sugar 900 grams
6 pints water   3.5 litres

1 tsp. citric acid
½ tsp. tannin
pectic enzyme
Campden tablets
nutrient
Champagne yeast

1   Top, tail and wash the gooseberries and pour 5 pints (3 litres) of boiling water on to them in a mashing bin.
2   When cool, crush the now soft berries with your hands, add the acid, tannin, pectic enzyme and 1 crushed Campden tablet.
3   Next day stir in the grape juice concentrate, nutrient and yeast.
4   Ferment on the pulp for 7 days, stirring twice daily.
5   Strain out the fruit, pressing it dry, stir in the sugar, pour the must into a fermentation jar, top up, fit an air-lock and continue fermentation to dryness.

70 GOOSEBERRY (sparkling)

Ingredients and method as for Recipe No. 69.
When the wine is six months old and star bright bottle it in Champagne bottles as described on page 65.
This makes an excellent sparkling wine after 1 year in bottle.

71 GRAPE
(dry white) I

11 lb white grapes   5 kg   Hock yeast
sugar, if necessary

English grown grapes may be used for this wine.
1   Remove the grapes from their stalks and crush each one.
2   Check the S.G. of the juice and if necessary stir in sufficient sugar to achieve S.G. 1.085.
3   Add an active yeast and ferment for 24 hours.
4   Press the grapes until all the juice is extracted and you have a jar full of must.
5   Fit an air-lock and continue fermentation to dryness.

72 GRAPE
(dry red)

11 lb black grapes   5 kg   Burgundy yeast
sugar, if necessary

1   Remove the grapes from their stalks and crush each one.
2   Check the S.G. of the juice and if necessary stir in sufficient sugar to achieve S.G. 1.090.
3   Ferment on the pulp for 14 days, stirring the must twice daily.
4   Strain and press the grapes until all the juice is extracted and you have a jar full of must.
5   Fit an air-lock and continue fermentation to dryness.

73 GRAPE (dry white) II

11 lb seedless Cypriot
grapes   5 kg
9 oz sugar   250 grams

1 tsp. citric acid
Campden tablets
Hock yeast

1. Stalk and sort the grapes, removing those that are bad or mouldy. Wash, drain and crush them, add the citric acid and 2 crushed Campden tablets, cover and leave for 48 hours.
2. Check the S.G. of the juice and if necessary stir in sufficient sugar to achieve S.G. 1.085.
3. Add the yeast and ferment on the pulp for 2 days.
4. Strain and press the grapes till all the juice is extracted and you have a full jar. Fit an air-lock and continue fermentation to dryness.

74 GRAPE (sweet)

Any of the three previous recipes can be made into a sweet wine by increasing the quantity of grapes by 2¼ lb (1 kg) and by adding sufficient sugar to increase the S.G. to 1.110. When the S.G. falls to 1.020 rack into a clean jar containing 2 crushed Campden tablets.

75 GRAPE (rosé)

11 lb fresh grapes
(either black or black
and white mixed) 5 kg

sugar, if necessary

Make as for Recipe No. 73 but terminate fermentation at S.G. 1.006 by racking into a clean jar containing 2 crushed Campden tablets.

76 GRAPE & APPLE ROSÉ

4½ lb black grapes 2 kg
15 lb mixed windfall
  apples 7 kg
5 lb sugar 2 kg
5 pints water 3 litres
1 tsp. citric acid

½ tsp. tannin
pectic enzyme
Campden tablets
nutrient
Champagne yeast

1 Put 4 pints (2 litres) of cold water in a mashing bin and stir in the citric acid and 1 crushed Campden tablet, the pectic enzyme and tannin.
2 Wash, stalk and crush the grapes and add to the water.
3 Wash and crush the apples and add to the water to avoid browning.
4 Cover the vessel and leave for 24 hours.
5 Stir in enough sugar to raise the S.G. of the must to 1.090 and add the nutrient and an active yeast.
6 Ferment on the pulp for 7 days, stirring twice daily.
7 Strain and press the pulp till dry, pour into fermentation jars and continue fermentation under an air-lock.
8 When S.G. 1.006 is reached, rack into clean jars and add 2 crushed Campden tablets to terminate fermentation.
Note: For a gardener with a few apple trees and a few vines this is a splendid way of using the crop. 12 bottles of an excellent rosé wine is produced.

Although this recipe is for a double quantity of wine the fruit creates a great deal of liquid, hence the relatively small amount of water.

77 GRAPE JUICE CONCENTRATE (red and white)

You can make a comprehensive range of wines from the various cans of grape juice concentrate now available. The recipe for each wine is printed on the label supplied with the can and should be followed in accordance with the manufacturer's instructions. See also pages 67–72.

78 GREENGAGE (dry)

$4\frac{1}{2}$ lb greengages
   suitable for cooking 2 kg
$\frac{1}{2}$ pint white grape juice
   concentrate 250 grams
2 lb sugar   900 grams
6 pints water   3.5 litres

1 tsp. citric acid
$\frac{1}{2}$ tsp. tannin
pectic enzyme
Campden tablets
nutrient
Chablis yeast

1   Wash and stalk the greengages, place them in a mashing bin and pour on boiling water.

2   When cool, mash the fruit and remove the stones. Stir in the acid, tannin, pectic enzyme and 1 crushed Campden tablet. Cover and leave for 24 hours.

3   Stir in the grape juice concentrate, nutrient and an active yeast, and ferment on the pulp for 5 days stirring twice daily.

4   Strain and press the fruit, stir in the sugar, pour into a fermentation jar, fit an air-lock and ferment to dryness.

79 GREENGAGE, CANNED

1 A$2\frac{1}{2}$ size can
   greengages   1 kg

$\frac{1}{2}$ pint white grape juice
   concentrate 250 grams

Other ingredients and method as for Recipe No. 21.
Note: Remove all the stones.

80 GRAPEFRUIT

4 large fresh grapefruit
$\frac{1}{2}$ pint white grape juice
   concentrate 250 grams
2 lb sugar   900 grams

6 pints water   3.5 litres
Campden tablets
nutrient
Hock yeast

1   Thinly pare the grapefruit and place the skin in a mashing bin.

2   Cut each grapefruit in half, squeeze out all the juice and add to the parings.

3   Add 6 pints (3.5 litres) cold water and 1 crushed Campden tablet, cover and leave till next day.

4   Stir in the grape juice concentrate, sugar, nutrient and

yeast and ferment for 5 days.

5   Strain out the parings, pour into a fermentation jar, top up and continue fermentation to S.G. 1.004.

6   Rack into a clean jar containing 2 crushed Campden tablets to terminate fermentation.

Note : No acid or tannin are necessary. Be careful to avoid all white pith from the fruit since this causes an unpleasant bitterness in the wine. Because of its high acidity this wine is best served not too dry.

81 GRAPEFRUIT CANNED

1 A2½ size can
grapefruit segments
    1 kg
½ pint white grape juice
concentrate 250 grams
2 lb sugar   900 grams

5 pints water   3 litres
½ tsp. tannin
pectic enzyme
Campden tablets
nutrient
Hock yeast

Make as for Recipe No. 21.

1 quart size can of
grapefruit juice 1 litre

82 GRAPEFRUIT JUICE, CANNED

Other ingredients and method as for Recipe No. 104.

Some out of season ingredients
Dried and canned fruits, honey and cereals enable us to make wine throughout the year. Use the syrup as well as the fruit.

83
HAWTHORNBERRY
(dry)

4 pints dry hawthorn berries 2¼ litre measure
½ pint white grape juice concentrate 250 grams
2 lb white sugar 900 grams

7 pints water 4 litres
½ oz citric acid 15 grams
pectic enzyme
Campden tablets
G.P. yeast

1 Wash the berries free from dust and leaves, shake them dry. Measure them in a suitable glass or jug, shake them down lightly and then place them in a mashing bin.
2 Pour 5 pints (3 litres) boiling water over the berries and when cool crush them with your hands and add the acid, pectic enzyme and 1 crushed Campden tablet.
3 Next day stir in the grape juice concentrate, nutrient and yeast and stir twice daily for 5 days.
4 Strain out the berries, stir in the sugar, pour into a fermentation jar, top up, fit an air-lock and continue fermentation to S.G. 1.006.
5 Rack into a clean jar and add 2 crushed Campden tablets to terminate fermentation.

84 HAWTHORN
BLOSSOM

1 quart fresh hawthorn blossoms, pink or white, free from leaf,

calix and other greenery, and lightly pressed down 1 litre

Other ingredients and method as for Recipe No. 42.

85 LEMON

10 small lemons
½ pint white grape juice
   concentrate 250 grams
2 lb sugar   900 grams
6 pints water   3.5 litres

2 tsp. glycerine
½ tsp. tannin
Campden tablets
nutrient
Sauternes yeast

1   Thinly pare the lemons, then cut them and squeeze out the juice.
2   Dissolve the sugar and grape juice concentrate in 5 pints (3 litres) of tepid water, add the tannin, lemon rind, lemon juice, nutrient and yeast.
3   Pour into a fermentation jar, top up, fit an air-lock and ferment to S.G. 1.008.
4   Rack into a clean jar containing 2 crushed Campden tablets and the 2 tsp. glycerine.
Note: No acid is required. The glycerine gives the wine a sweetish taste which masks the high acidity from the lemons.

86 LETTUCE

2¼ lb chopped lettuce
   of strong flavour, such
   as a cos   1 kg
½ pint white grape juice
   concentrate 250 grams
2 lb white sugar
                900 grams

6 pints water   3.5 litres
½ oz citric acid 15 grams
½ tsp. tannin
Campden tablets
nutrient
Hock yeast

1   Wash the lettuce, chop it into small pieces and boil it gently for ten minutes in 4 pints (2 litres) of water.
2   Strain the liquid on to the sugar and when cool add the grape juice concentrate, acid, tannin, nutrient and yeast.
3   Pour into a fermentation jar, top up, fit an air-lock and ferment to dryness.

87 LOGANBERRY
(dry)

2¼ lb ripe loganberries 1 kg
½ pint red grape juice
  concentrate 250 grams
2 lb sugar   900 grams
6 pints water 3.5 litres

½ tsp. citric acid
¼ tsp. tannin
pectic enzyme
Campden tablets
Burgundy yeast

1   Stalk and rinse the loganberries free from leaves and dust, pour 5 pints (3 litres) of boiling water onto them and leave covered till cool.
2   Stir in the acid, tannin, pectic enzyme and 1 crushed Campden tablet, cover and leave for 24 hours.
3   Stir in the grape juice concentrate, nutrient and yeast, and ferment on the pulp for 7 days, stirring twice daily.
4   Strain out the fruit, stir in the sugar, pour into a fermentation jar, top up, fit an air-lock and ferment to dryness.

88 LOGANBERRY
(sweet)

2¾ lb loganberries
          2.25 kg
½ pint red grape juice
  concentrate
          250 grams
2¾ lb sugar   1.1 kg
6 pints water 3.5 litres

½ tsp. citric acid
½ tsp. tannin
pectic enzyme
Campden tablets
nutrient
Port yeast

1   Prepare as for Recipe No. 87 but add only half the sugar at first and the remainder in three equal doses at 8 day intervals.
2   When S.G. 1.020 has been reached after all the sugar has been added, rack into a clean jar containing 2 crushed Campden tablets.

89 LOGANBERRY, CANNED

1 A2½ size can loganberries   1 kg
½ pint red grape juice concentrate 250 grams
2 lb sugar   900 grams
5 pints water   3 litres

1 tsp. citric acid
½ tsp. tannin
pectic enzyme
Campden tablets
nutrient
Burgundy yeast

Make as for Recipe No. 21.

90 MAIZE

1 pint crushed maize   500 grams
1 pint white grape juice concentrate 500 grams
2¾ lb sugar   1 kg
5 pints water   3 litres

½ oz citric acid 15 grams
½ tsp. tannin
fungal amylase
nutrient
Tokay yeast

1   Use crushed or minced maize, wash it free from dust and place it in a mashing bin.
2   Pour on 5 pints (3 litres) of boiling water and leave to cool.
3   Stir in the fungal amylase as directed on the packet together with the acid and tannin. Leave for 24 hours.
4   Next day stir in the grape juice concentrate, nutrient and yeast, and ferment for 5 days, stirring twice daily.
5   Strain out the maize, stir in the sugar, pour into a fermentation jar, top up, fit an air-lock and continue fermentation.
6   Finish the wine sweet, around S.G. 1.010 or a little higher.

91 MANDARIN ORANGES, CANNED

1 A2½ size can of
  mandarin oranges 1 kg
½ pint white grape juice
  concentrate 250 grams
2 lb white sugar 900 grams
5 pints water   3 litres

½ tsp. citric acid
½ tsp. tannin
pectic enzyme
Campden tablets
nutrient
Chablis yeast

Make as for Recipe No. 21.

92 MANGO

1 A2½ size can mango
  slices   1 kg
½ pint grape juice
  concentrate 250 grams
2 lb sugar   900 grams
6 pints water 3.5 litres

½ oz citric acid 15 grams
½ tsp. tannin
pectic enzyme
Campden tablets
nutrient
G.P. yeast

Make as for Recipe No. 21.

93 MANGOLD (sweet)

4½ lb mangolds   2 kg
½ pint grape juice
  concentrate 250 grams
2¾ lb sugar   1.1 kg
7 pints water   4 litres

¾ oz citric acid
            20 grams
½ tsp. tannin
nutrient
G.P. yeast

Make as for Recipe No. 20 but omit the spices.

94 MARROW
(sweet)

4½ lb ripe marrow   2 kg
½ pint white grape juice
   concentrate 500 grams
2¼ lb sugar   1 kg
4 pints water   2 litres
½ oz whole ginger
              15 grams

6 cloves
¾ oz citric acid
              20 grams
½ tsp. tannin
Campden tablets
nutrient
G.P. yeast

1 Wipe the marrow clean and grate it into a mashing bin. Don't crush the seeds but include them and the rind.
2 Pour on 4 pints (2 litres) boiling water and when cool stir in the grape juice concentrate, spices, acid, tannin, nutrient and yeast.
3 Ferment on the pulp for 4 days, stirring twice daily.
4 Strain out the solids, stir in the sugar, pour into a fermentation jar, top up, fit an air-lock and ferment to S.G. 1.020.
5 Rack into a clean jar containing 2 crushed Campden tablets to terminate fermentation. Later, fine and filter.

95 MEDLAR
(sweet)

4½ lb ripe medlars free
   from green   2 kg
½ pint white grape juice
   concentrate 250 grams
2¼ lb sugar   1 kg
5 pints water   3 litres

2 tsp. citric acid
½ tsp. tannin
pectic enzyme
Campden tablets
nutrient
Sauternes yeast

1 Wash and crush the medlars and drop them into a mashing bin and pour onto them 4 pints (2 litres) boiling water.
2 When cool add the acid, tannin, pectic enzyme and 1 crushed Campden tablet.
3 Next day stir in the grape juice concentrate, nutrient and yeast, and ferment on the pulp for 5 days, stirring

twice daily.

4   Strain out the fruit, stir in the sugar, pour into a fermentation jar, top up, fit an air-lock and ferment to S.G. 1.016.

5   Rack into a clean jar containing 2 crushed Campden tablets.

6   2 weeks later fine and filter then store and mature.

96 MIXED FRESH FRUIT (dry)

$3\frac{1}{4}$ lb mixed summer fruit as available (red, white and black currants, cherries, raspberries, logan-berries, stawberries, gooseberries, early plums, etc.)   1.5 kg
$\frac{1}{2}$ pint red or white grape juice concentrate
250 grams

2 lb sugar   900 grams
5 pints water   3 litres
$\frac{1}{2}$ tsp. citric acid
$\frac{1}{2}$ tsp. tannin
pectic enzyme
Campden tablets
nutrient
Champagne yeast

1   Wash and clean the fruit, discarding stalks and stones.

2   Pour on 4 pints (2 litres) hot water and when cool, mash the fruit.

3   Add the acid, tannin, pectic enzyme, nutrient and 1 crushed Campden tablet. Cover and leave for 24 hours.

4   Stir in the grape juice concentrate, nutrient and yeast.

5   Ferment on the pulp for 5 days, stirring twice daily.

6   Strain out the fruit, stir in the sugar, pour into a fermentation jar, top up, fit an air-lock and ferment to S.G. 1.004.

7   Rack into a clean jar containing 2 crushed Campden tablets to terminate fermentation. Rack again in 4 weeks.

Some fruit suitable for wine making Apples, pears, plums, oranges, lemons, bananas, grapefruit, rhubarb and above all grapes. Use the best you can get.

97 MIXED FRESH FRUIT (sweet)

4 lb fruit as for Recipe No. 96   1.75 kg

2¾ lb sugar   1.25 kg
Port yeast

Other ingredients and method as for Recipe No. 96, but add only 1 lb (500 grams) sugar at first and the remainder in 3 equal doses at 8 day intervals. Ferment the wine as long as possible and finish it sweet at about S.G. 1.020. Rack and store for 1 year before bottling.

98 MIXED DRIED FRUIT (dry)

2¼ lb mixed currants, raisins and sultanas   1 kg
½ pint white grape juice concentrate 250 grams
9 oz brown sugar   250 grams

7 pints water   4 litres
2 tsp. citric acid
½ tsp. tannin
pectic enzyme
Campden tablets
nutrient
Madeira yeast

Make as for Recipe No. 128.

99 MIXED DRIED FRUIT (sweet)

2¾ lb mixed dried fruit   1.25 kg

18 oz brown sugar   500 grams

Other ingredients as Recipe No. 98.
Make as for Recipe No. 129.

100 MULBERRY (dry)

2¾ lb fresh ripe
mulberries   1 kg
½ pint red grape juice
concentrate 250 grams
2 lb sugar   900 grams
6 pints water   3.5 litres

1 tsp. citric acid
½ tsp. tannin
pectic enzyme
Campden tablets
nutrient
Burgundy yeast

1 Wash and stalk the fruit and pour on 5 pints (3 litres) of hot water.
2 When cool add the acid, tannin, pectic enzyme and 1 crushed Campden tablet. Cover and leave for 24 hours.
3 Stir in the grape juice concentrate, nutrient and yeast, and ferment on the pulp for 5 days, stirring twice daily.
4 Strain out the fruit, stir in the sugar, pour into a fermentation jar, top up, fit an air-lock and ferment to dryness.

101 MULBERRY (sweet)

2¾ lb mulberries 1.25 kg
½ pint red grape juice
concentrate 250 grams

2½ lb sugar   1.1 kg
Sauternes yeast

Other ingredients and method as for Recipe No. 100, but terminate fermentation at S.G. 1.016 by racking into a clean jar containing 2 crushed Campden tablets.

102 ORANGE (dry)

4 Seville and 4 sweet oranges
½ pint white grape juice concentrate 250 grams
2¼ lb white sugar   1 kg

7 pints water   4 litres
½ tsp. tannin
nutrient
Sherry yeast

1   Very thinly pare the oranges so that no white pith is removed.
2   Place the skins in a mashing bin together with the sugar and pour on 5 pints (3 litres) boiling water. Stir well.
3   When cool stir in the grape juice concentrate, the expressed juice of the oranges, the tannin, nutrient and yeast.
4   Ferment for 3 days, stirring daily, then strain out the skins.
5   Pour into a fermentation jar, top up, fit an air-lock and ferment to dryness.

Note : No acid is required. This wine is best made in January.

103 ORANGE (sweet)

5 Seville and 5 sweet oranges
½ pint grape juice concentrate 250 grams
2½ lb sugar   1.1 kg

7 pints water   4 litres
½ tsp. tannin
Campden tablets
nutrient
Sauternes yeast

Make as for Recipe No. 102 but rack at S.G. 1.020 and add 2 crushed Campden tablets.

104 ORANGE JUICE, CANNED AND UNSWEETENED

1 19 oz can orange
  juice   1 litre
½ pint white grape juice
  concentrate 250 grams
2 lb sugar   900 grams
5 pints water   3 litres

1 tsp. glycerine
½ tsp. tannin
Campden tablets
nutrient
G.P. yeast

1 Stir all the ingredients into 5 pints (3 litres) tepid water until the sugar is dissolved.
2 Pour into a fermentation jar, top up, fit an air-lock and ferment to S.G. 1.002.
3 Rack into a clean jar containing 2 crushed Campden tablets to terminate fermentation so that this wine can be served not quite dry.

105 PARSLEY

1 lb fresh young parsley
  leaves   500 grams
½ pint white grape juice
  concentrate 250 grams
2 lb white sugar
         900 grams

7 pints water   4 litres
½ oz citric acid
         15 grams
½ tsp. tannin
nutrient
Chablis yeast

1 Wash the parsley, then simmer it in 5 pints (3 litres) water for 20 minutes.
2 Strain on to the sugar, acid and tannin. Stir well and leave to cool.
3 Stir in the grape juice concentrate, nutrient and yeast.
4 Pour into a fermentation jar, top up, fit an air-lock and ferment to dryness.

106 PARSNIP
(dry)

4 lb parsnips   1.75 kg
½ pint white grape juice
   concentrate 250 grams
2 lb sugar   900 grams
7 pints water   4 litres

½ oz citric acid 15 grams
½ tsp. tannin
nutrient
G.P. yeast

1   Scrub the parsnips clean from every trace of soil and rust. Cut off and discard the base of the leaves, dice the stems.
2   Boil the diced parsnips until they are tender and if you so wish use them as a vegetable for a meal.
3   Strain the liquor on to the sugar, acid and tannin. Stir well.
4   When cool stir in the grape juice concentrate, nutrient and yeast. Pour into a fermentation jar, top up, fit an air-lock and ferment to dryness.
Note: It is best to make this wine in January after the parsnips have been well frosted since this improves the flavour. It is not necessary to peel or core them.

107 PARSNIP
(sweet)

4½ lb parsnips   2 kg
½ pint white grape juice
   concentrate 250 grams
2½ lb brown sugar
   1.1 kg

7 pints water   4 litres
½ oz citric acid 15 grams
½ tsp. tannin
nutrient
Madeira yeast

Make as for Recipe No. 106 but add only half the sugar at first and the remainder in 3 equal doses at 8 day intervals. Ferment as long as possible and finish the wine sweet at S.G. 1.020.

108 PEACH (dry)

3¼ lb ripe peaches
           1.5 kg
½ pint white grape juice
   concentrate 250 grams
2 lb sugar   900 grams
6 pints water   3.5 litres

2 tsp. citric acid
½ tsp. tannin
pectic enzyme
Campden tablets
nutrient
G.P. yeast

1   Split the peaches, remove and discard the stones.
2   Pour 5 pints (3 litres) hot water over the peaches and when cool mash them with your hands.
3   Stir in the acid, tannin, pectic enzyme and 1 Campden tablet.
4   Next day stir in the grape juice concentrate, nutrient and yeast and ferment on the pulp for 4 days, stirring twice daily.
5   Strain out the fruit, stir in the sugar, pour into a fermentation jar, top up, fit an air-lock and ferment to dryness.

Note: Many people prefer this wine not quite dry and you may wish to rack at S.G. 1.002 and add 2 crushed Campden tablets to terminate fermentation.

109 PEACH (sweet)

3 lb 14 oz ripe peaches
           1.75 kg
½ pint white grape juice
   concentrate 250 grams

2½ lb white sugar 1.1 kg
Sauternes yeast

Other ingredients and method as for Recipe No. 108, but finish the wine sweet by racking at S.G. 1.020 and adding 2 crushed Campden tablets.

110 PEACH PULP

1 A2½ size can peach pulp   1 kg
1 pint white grape juice concentrate 500 grams
pectic enzyme
Campden tablets

4½ lb sugar   2 kg
11 pints water   6 litres
1 oz citric acid 25 grams
1 tsp. tannin
nutrient
Sauternes yeast

1 Empty the contents of the can into a saucepan, add 1 quart (1 litre) water and boil gently for 15 minutes.
2 Empty the saucepan into a mashing bin, add 4 pints (2 litres) cold water, the acid, tannin, pectic enzyme and 1 crushed Campden tablet.
3 Cover and leave for 2 days in a warm place.
4 Stir in the grape juice concentrate, nutrient and yeast and ferment on the pulp for 3 days, stirring twice daily.
5 Strain out the pulp, stir in the sugar and top up to 2 gallons (9 litres) with cold boiled water.
6 Ferment to S.G. 1.010, then rack and add 2 crushed Campden tablets.
7 2 weeks later, fine and filter, then store for 6 months.

Note: This makes 12 bottles of a very good sweet table wine, and matures fairly quickly.

111 PEAPOD (dry)

3¼ lb fresh young pea pods after the shelling of the peas   1.5 kg
½ pint white grape juice concentrate 250 grams
2 lb sugar   900 grams

7 pints water   4 litres
2 tsp. citric acid
½ tsp. tannin
nutrient
Hock yeast

1 Boil the pods in 4 pints (2 litres) of water until they are tender.
2 Strain the liquor onto the sugar, acid and tannin, and stir well.
3 When cool, add the grape juice concentrate, nutrient

and yeast.

4 Pour into a fermentation jar, top up, fit an air-lock and ferment to dryness.

112 PEAR (dry)

4½ lb cooking pears or dessert pears not quite ripe	2 kg	7 pints water	4 litres
½ pint white grape juice concentrate	250 grams	2 tsp. citric acid	
2 lb sugar	900 grams	pectic enzyme	
		Campden tablets	
		nutrient	
		Champagne yeast	

Make as for Recipe No. 1 but do not include tannin.

113 PEAR (sweet)

5¼ lb pears	2.5 kg	Sauternes yeast
2¼ lb sugar	1.1 kg	

Other ingredients and method as for Recipe No. 2 but omit tannin.

114 PEAR (sparkling)

Ingredients as for Recipe No. 112 and method as for Recipe No. 1. When wine is 6 months old and quite clear, rack into clean champagne bottles and add sugar and active yeast as described on page 65. This is a superb sparkling wine.

115 PEAR & PLUM

5½ lb mixed pears and plums, no stones	2.5 kg	½ pint red grape juice concentrate	250 grams

Other ingredients as for Recipe No. 112 and method as for Recipe No. 1.

116 PEAR & APPLE

9 lb mixed cooking apples and pears 4 kg

½ pint white grape juice concentrate 250 grams

Other ingredients as for Recipe No. 112.
Method as for Recipe No. 1.
In many gardens a windfall of apples, pears and plums comes together. These recipes indicate to you how to make good use of them and the wine should be made in large quantities.

117 PINEAPPLE

4 fresh pineapples
½ pint white grape juice
concentrate 250 grams
2¼ lb white sugar 1 kg
7 pints water 4 litres

2 tsp. citric acid
½ tsp. tannin
Campden tablets
nutrient
G.P. yeast

1 Wash, top and tail the pineapples but do not peel them.
2 Chop them up into small cubes and boil them in 4 pints (2 litres) water for 15 minutes.
3 Strain on to the sugar, acid and tannin, and stir well.
4 When cool add the grape juice concentrate, nutrient and an active yeast.
5 Pour into a fermentation jar, top up, fit an air-lock and ferment to S.G. 1.004.
6 Rack and add 2 crushed Campden tablets to terminate fermentation.

118 PINEAPPLE JUICE, CANNED

1 19 oz can pineapple juice 1 litre

Other ingredients and method as for Recipe No. 104.

138

119 PLUM (dry)

4½ lb red/black fresh plums — 2 kg
½ pint red grape juice concentrate — 250 grams
2 lb sugar — 900 grams
6 pints water — 3.5 litres

1 tsp. citric acid
½ tsp. tannin
pectic enzyme
Campden tablets
nutrient
Bordeaux yeast

1   Wash the plums in hot water to remove the waxy bloom and place them in a mashing bin.
2   Pour on 5 pints (3 litres) boiling water to soften the plums and leave to cool.
3   Mash the plums and remove the stones.
4   Stir in the acid, tannin, pectic enzyme and 1 Campden tablet.
5   Next day, stir in the grape juice concentrate, nutrient and an active yeast.
6   Ferment on the pulp for 5 days, stirring twice daily.
7   Strain out the fruit, stir in the sugar, pour into a fermentation jar, top up, fit an air-lock and ferment till dry.

120 PLUM (sweet)

6 lb plums of mixed varieties if possible — 2.75 kg
½ pint red grape juice concentrate — 250 grams
2½ lb sugar — 1.1 kg
6 pints water — 3.5 litres

1 tsp. citric acid
½ tsp. tannin
pectic enzyme
Campden tablets
nutrient
Port yeast

Make as for Recipe No. 119, but use only half the sugar at first and add the remainder in 3 equal doses at 8 day intervals. Ferment for as long as possible and finish this strong wine sweet at about S.G. 1.020.

121 PLUM, VICTORIA

6 lb Victoria plums
          2. 75kg
$\frac{1}{2}$ pint white grape juice
   concentrate 250 grams
$2\frac{1}{2}$ lb sugar   1.1 kg
6 pints water   3.5 litres

1 tsp. citric acid
$\frac{1}{2}$ tsp. tannin
pectic enzyme
Campden tablets
nutrient
Sherry yeast

Make as for Recipe No. 119, but continue fermentation as long as possible and add extra sugar if necessary. Ferment down to S.G. 1.006 and mature in a jar plugged with cotton wool. When fully mature this is a splendid wine.

122 PLUM & APPLE

6 lb mixed cooking
   apples and plums
          2.75 kg
1 tsp. citric acid
$\frac{1}{2}$ tsp. tannin
pectic enzyme

$\frac{1}{2}$ pint red grape juice
   concentrate 250 grams
2 lb sugar   900 grams
Campden tablets
nutrient
G.P. yeast

Make as for Recipe No. 1. This is another good everyday wine.

123 PLUM, CANNED I

1 A$2\frac{1}{2}$ size can golden
   plums   1 kg
$\frac{1}{2}$ pint white grape juice
   concentrate 250 grams
2 lb sugar   900 grams
5 pints water   3 litres

2 tsp. citric acid
$\frac{1}{2}$ tsp. tannin
pectic enzyme
Campden tablets
nutrient
Chablis yeast

Make as for Recipe No. 21, but remove any stones.

124 PLUM, CANNED II

Other plums, plum pulps and plum pie fillings are available. Use red grape juice concentrate with red fruit.
Other ingredients as for Recipe No. 123 and method as for No. 21.

125 POTATO

$2\frac{1}{4}$ lb old potatoes   1 kg
$2\frac{1}{2}$ lb chopped raisins
                      1 kg
1 lb crushed wheat
              500 grams
$1\frac{1}{2}$ lb sugar – brown if
   possible   700 grams

7 pints water   4 litres
$\frac{1}{2}$ oz tartaric acid
                  15 grams
$\frac{1}{2}$ tsp. tannin
fungal amylase
nutrient
Cereal or Madeira yeast

1 Scrub the potatoes clean from every trace of soil, chop them into small cubes and place them in a mashing bin.
2 Wash the wheat free from dust, crush it and add to the bin.
3 Wash and chop the raisins, avoid breaking any pips, add to the bin.
4 Pour on 7 pints (4 litres) water that is on the boil, and stir well.
5 When cool add the acid, tannin, fungal amylase, nutrient and an active yeast.
6 Ferment on the pulp for 7 days, stirring twice daily.
7 Strain out the solids, stir in half the sugar, pour into a fermentation jar and ferment for 10 days.
8 Add the remainder of the sugar in two doses at 8 day intervals.
9 Ferment as long as possible adding more sugar if necessary.
10 Finish fermentation about S.G. 1.020 and keep this very strong sweet wine for 3 years so that it can mature fully. A long wait but well worth it.

126 PRUNE

$2\frac{1}{4}$ lb best dried prunes
                      1 kg
$\frac{1}{2}$ pint white grape juice
   concentrate 250 grams
$2\frac{1}{4}$ lb sugar   1 kg
7 pints water   4 litres

2 tsp. citric acid
$\frac{1}{2}$ tsp. tannin
pectic enzyme
Campden tablets
nutrient
Sherry yeast

Make as for Recipe No. 13.

127 QUINCE

4½ lb ripe and mellow
  quince   2 kg
½ pint white grape juice
  concentrate 250 grams
2 lb sugar   900 grams
5 pints water   3 litres

2 tsp. citric acid
½ tsp. tannin
pectic enzyme
Campden tablets
nutrient
Champagne yeast

1   Wash and quarter the quinces, remove the cores and crush the fruit, then continue as for Recipe No. 2.

128 RAISIN (dry)

2¼ lb best raisins   1 kg
½ pint white grape juice
  concentrate 250 grams
8 pints water   4.5 litres
2 tsp. citric acid

½ tsp. tannin
Campden tablets
nutrient
Hock yeast

1   Wash the raisins in water containing a little citric acid and 1 crushed Campden tablet, drain them, chop them not breaking any pips, and place them in a mashing bin.
2   Pour on 7 pints (4 litres) boiling water, and leave to cool.
3   Stir in the acid, tannin, nutrient and yeast, and ferment on the pulp for 7 days, stirring twice daily.
4   Strain out and press the raisins, stir in the grape juice concentrate, pour into a fermentation jar, top up, fit an air-lock and ferment to dryness.

129 RAISIN
(sweet)

2¾ lb best raisins
               1.25 kg
½ pint white grape juice
  concentrate 250 grams
9 oz sugar   250 grams
7 pints water   4 litres

2 tsp. citric acid
½ tsp. tannin
Campden tablets
nutrient
Sauternes yeast

Make as for Recipe No. 128. Add the sugar with the grape juice concentrate and when S.G. 1.020 is reached about 10 days later, terminate fermentation by racking and adding 2 crushed Campden tablets.

130 RAISIN,
MUSCATEL

4 lb muscatel raisins
               1.8 kg
9 oz soft brown sugar
          250 grams
7 pints water   4 litres
2 tsp. citric acid

½ tsp. tannin
pectic enzyme
Campden tablets
nutrient
Sherry yeast

1   Wash, drain and chop the muscatels, place them in a bin and pour 7 pints (4 litres) boiling water on them.
2   When cool add the citric acid, tannin, pectic enzyme and 1 crushed Campden tablet. Cover and leave for 24 hours.
3   Next day add the nutrient and yeast and ferment on the pulp for 7 days, stirring twice daily.
4   Strain out the fruit, stir in the sugar, and pour into a fermentation jar. Fit an air-lock and ferment to S.G. 1.010, or ferment under a plug of cotton wool to enhance the sherry-like flavour.
5   Mature in jars not quite full to maintain a good sherry-like flavour. Keep for 1 year to mature.

131 RASPBERRY (dry)

2¾ lb ripe raspberries 1.25 kg
½ pint red grape juice concentrate 250 grams
2 lb sugar 900 grams
6 pints water 3.5 litres

pectic enzyme
Campden tablets
nutrient
G.P. yeast
No acid or tannin

1 Stalk and wash the raspberries, place them in a mashing bin and pour 5 pints (3 litres) hot water over them.
2 When cool mash them, add the pectic enzyme and 1 Campden tablet. Cover and leave for 24 hours.
3 Stir in the grape juice concentrate, nutrient and yeast and ferment on the pulp for 5 days, stirring twice daily.
4 Strain out the fruit, stir in the sugar, pour into a fermentation jar, top up, fit an air-lock and ferment to S.G. 1.002.
5 Rack into a clean jar and add 2 crushed Campden tablets to terminate fermentation since this wine is best when not too dry. Mature the wine for 1 year.

132 RASPBERRY (sweet)

Ingredients and method as for Recipe No. 131 but use 2½ lb (1.1 kg) sugar and rack at S.G. 1.016. It is unwise to use too many raspberries since there is a change of flavour during fermentation. The same is true of fresh strawberries.

133 RASPBERRY, CANNED

1 A2½ size can raspberries 1 kg
½ pint red grape juice concentrate 250 grams
2 lb sugar 900 grams
5 pints water 3 litres

pectic enzyme
Campden tablets
nutrient
G.P. yeast
No acid or tannin

Make as for Recipe No. 21.

144

**134
REDCURRANT**

3 lb redcurrants 1.4 kg
½ pint red grape juice
  concentrate 250 grams
2 lb sugar 900 grams
6 pints water 3.5 litres
½ tsp. tannin

pectic enzyme
Campden tablets
nutrient
Bordeaux yeast
No acid required

1   Remove the stalks and wash the fruit, mash it and pour
     on 5 pints (3 litres) boiling water.
2   Continue as in Recipe No. 131.

135 RHUBARB

4½ lb rhubarb 2 kg
½ pint white grape juice
  concentrate 250 grams
2 lb sugar 900 grams
6 pints water 3.5 litres
1 lemon, thinly pared rind

½ tsp. tannin
pectic enzyme
Campden tablets
nutrient
G.P. yeast

1   Use garden rhubarb freshly gathered in May or early
     June. Forced and end-of-season rhubarbs are un-
     suitable. Remove the top inch or two (2 or 3 cm) of
     stalk with the leaf and the white portion at the bottom.
     Wipe the stalks clean and chop them into small pieces.
2   Place them in a mashing bin, add the thinly pared rind
     of the lemon, (the juice is NOT required) and pour on
     5 pints (3 litres) boiling water.
3   When cool add the pectic enzyme and 1 crushed
     Campden tablet, cover and leave for 24 hours.
4   Stir in the grape juice concentrate, tannin, nutrient and
     yeast and ferment on the pulp for 5 days, stirring twice
     daily.
5   Strain out the fruit, stir in the sugar, pour into a
     fermentation jar, top up, fit an air-lock and ferment to
     S.G. 1.002.
6   Rack and add 2 crushed Campden tablets.
Note : Because of the high acidity this wine tastes better
     not quite dry.

136 RHUBARB (sweet)

5½ lb rhubarb   2.5 kg
½ pint white grape juice
   concentrate 250 grams

2½ lb sugar   1.1 kg

Other ingredients and method as for Recipe No. 135 but rack at S.G. 1.016 and add 2 Campden tablets to terminate fermentation.

137 RICE & RAISIN

1 lb crushed rice
   500 grams
1 lb chopped raisins
   500 grams
½ pint white grape juice
   concentrate 250 grams
1¾ lb sugar 800 grams

7 pints water 4 litres
2 tsp. citric acid
½ tsp. tannin
Campden tablets
nutrient
Cereal yeast

1   Wash the rice and raisins and then crush the one and chop the other and place them in a mashing bin.
2   Pour on 5 pints (3 litres) boiling water and when cool stir in the grape juice concentrate, acid, tannin, nutrient and yeast.
3   Ferment for 7 days stirring twice daily, then strain out the solids, stir in the sugar, pour into a fermentation jar, top up, fit an air-lock and ferment to S.G. 1.006.
4   Rack and add 2 crushed Campden tablets to terminate fermentation.

138 ROSEHIP (dry)

9 oz rosehip shells
   250 grams
½ pint white grape juice
   concentrate 250 grams
2 lb sugar 900 grams
7 pints water 4 litres

1 tsp. citric acid
½ tsp. tannin
Campden tablets
nutrient
Sherry yeast

Wash the rosehip shells free from dust, pour boiling water on to them and continue as for Recipe No. 137, but allow to ferment right out.

146

139 ROSEHIP
(sweet)

9 oz rosehip shells
        250 grams
½ pint white grape juice
concentrate 250 grams

2½ lb sugar   1.1 kg

Other ingredients as for Recipe No. 138 and method as for 137, but terminate fermentation at S.G. 1.012.

140 ROSEHIP
& FIG

9 oz rosehip shells
        250 grams
7 oz figs   200 grams
½ pint white grape juice
concentrate 250 grams
2¾ lb sugar   1.25 kg

7 pints water   4 litres
2 tsp. citric acid
½ tsp. tannin
nutrient
Sherry yeast

1 Wash the rosehip shells, break up the figs and boil them both in 6 pints (3.5 litres) water for 15 minutes.
2 Strain and cool, then stir in the grape juice concentrate, the acid, tannin, nutrient and yeast. Ferment in a bin covered with a sheet of polythene fastened with a rubber band.
3 After 5 days stir in 1 lb (500 grams) of sugar. Stir in the rest of the sugar in 3 equal doses at 8 day intervals so as steadily to increase the alcoholic tolerance of the yeast.
4 When the last of the sugar is added, pour into a fermentation jar, top up, fit an air-lock and if possible ferment to dryness. Your wine will now be about 16% alcohol and will need 2 years to mature into a smooth, sherry-type wine that is excellent as an aperitif.

141 ROSEHIP SYRUP

12 fl oz (the standard bottle for this commodity) rosehip syrup 350 ml
½ pint white grape juice concentrate 250 grams
1¾ lb sugar 800 grams

6 pints water 3.5 litres
1 tsp. citric acid
½ tsp. tannin
Campden tablets
nutrient
Sauternes yeast

1 Mix all the ingredients together except the Campden tablets, pour into a standard fermentation jar, top up, fit an air-lock and ferment to S.G. 1.004.
2 Rack and add 2 crushed Campden tablets to terminate fermentation. This wine is best not quite dry.

142 ROSE PETAL

2 quarts red rose petals 2 litres

Other ingredients and method as for Recipe No. 42.

143 SLOE I (dry)

2¾ lb fresh ripe sloes 1.25 kg
½ pint red grape juice concentrate 250 grams
2 lb sugar 900 grams
6 pints water 3.5 litres

2 tsp. citric acid
½ tsp. tannin
pectic enzyme
Campden tablets
nutrient
Bordeaux yeast

1 Stalk and wash the sloes and pour on 5 pints (3 litres) boiling water, cover and leave to cool.
2 Mash the fruit, add the citric acid, tannin, pectic enzyme and 1 crushed Campden tablet. Cover and leave 1 day.
3 Stir in the grape juice concentrate, nutrient and yeast and ferment on the pulp for 5 days, stirring twice daily.
4 Strain out the fruit, stir in the sugar, pour into a fermentation jar, top up, fit an air-lock and ferment dry.

148

144 SLOE II
(sweet)

Ingredients and method as for Recipe No. 143 but use 2½ lb (1.1 kg) sugar, and terminate fermentation at S.G. 1.020 by racking and adding 2 Campden tablets.

145 SLOE III

Fresh sloes are not always easy to obtain and dried sloes do almost as well.

9 oz dried sloes 250 grams	2 tsp. citric acid
½ pint red grape juice concentrate 250 grams	½ tsp. tannin
	pectic enzyme
2 lb sugar 900 grams	nutrient
7 pints water 4 litres	Burgundy yeast

Make as for Recipe No. 22.

146 SLOE GIN

9 oz fresh ripe sloes
250 grams

4½ oz white sugar
125 grams
26 fl oz gin (1 bottle)

1 Stalk and wash the sloes, drain them dry and cut them in two lengthways.
2 Dissolve the sugar in the gin and pour it over the sloes.
3 Seal the jar and leave for 3 months but giving the bottle an occasional shake.
4 Strain off the sloe gin through a fine nylon sieve, pressing the fruit as dry as possible with a wooden spoon.
5 Bottle and serve as a liqueur at your convenience.

147 SLOE, BLACKBERRY & APPLE I

1 lb fresh sloes
500 grams
1 lb fresh blackberries
500 grams
1¾ lb sugar   800 grams
6 pints water   3.5 litres
1 tsp. citric acid
½ tsp. tannin

4½ lb mixed windfall
apples   2 kg
½ pint red grape juice
concentrate 250 grams
pectic enzyme
Campden tablets
nutrient
Bordeaux yeast

1   Stalk and wash the sloes and blackberries and pour 5 pints (3 litres) boiling water on them. Cover and leave to cool.
2   Add the acid, tannin, pectic enzyme and 1 crushed Campden tablet.
3   Wash the apples, remove any damaged parts, crush them and add them to the other fruit. Cover and leave 24 hours.
4   Stir in the grape juice concentrate, nutrient and yeast and ferment on the pulp for 7 days, stirring twice daily.
5   Strain and press the fruit, stir in the sugar, pour into a fermentation jar, top up, fit an air-lock and ferment to dryness.

Note: This is a good way to "stretch" the "red" fruits to make more red wine.

148 SLOE, BLACKBERRY & APPLE II

Ingredients and method as for Recipe No. 147 but use white grape juice concentrate and only ¼ tsp. tannin to make a rosé wine of excellent flavour. Terminate fermentation about S.G. 1.004 by racking and adding 2 crushed Campden tablets, so that the wine is not too dry.

149 SPINACH

2¼ lb spinach   1 kg
1 pint white grape juice
   concentrate 500 grams
18 oz sugar   500 grams
6 pints water   3.5 litres

2 tsp. citric acid
½ tsp. tannin
Campden tablets
nutrient
G.P. yeast

1   Wash and clean the spinach, then boil it in 5 pints (3 litres) water until it is cooked.
2   Strain off the liquor and press the spinach with a wooden spoon to extract as much juice as possible. It may be eaten as a vegetable at a meal.
3   Stir in the other ingredients except the Campden tablets, pour into a fermentation jar, top up, fit an air-lock and ferment to S.G. 1.004.
4   Rack and add 2 crushed Campden tablets to terminate fermentation. This wine is best when it is not too dry.

150 STRAWBERRY, CANNED

1 A2½ size can
   stawberries   1 kg
½ pint white grape juice
   concentrate 250 grams
1¾ lb white sugar
       800 grams

2 tsp. citric acid
½ tsp. tannin
pectic enzyme
Campden tablets
nutrient
Sauternes yeast

Make as for Recipe No. 21 but terminate fermentation by racking and adding 2 crushed Campden tablets when S.G. 1.004 is reached.

This is a very delicate rosé wine best served not too dry. An alternative is to use red grape juice concentrate and produce a wine of darker hue.

151
STRAWBERRY II

3 lb strawberry jam
              1.36 kg
$\frac{1}{2}$ pint white or red or
  mixture grape juice
  concentrate 250 grams
1 lb sugar   500 grams
7 pints water   4 litres

2 tsp. citric acid
$\frac{1}{2}$ tsp. tannin
pectic enzyme
  (double dose)
Campden tablets
nutrient
Sauternes yeast

1   Dissolve the jam in 5 pints (3 litres) warm water and when cool add the acid, tannin, pectic enzyme and 1 Campden tablet. Cover and leave for 2 days.
2   Stir in the grape juice concentrate, nutrient and yeast and ferment for 5 days, stirring twice daily.
3   Strain out the solids, stir in the sugar, pour into a fermentation jar, top up, fit an air-lock and ferment to S.G. 1.004.
4   Rack into a clean jar containing 2 crushed Campden tablets. This is a surprisingly attractive rosé wine.

152
STRAWBERRY III

12 fl oz (the standard
  bottle for this syrup)
  strawberry syrup
              350 ml
$\frac{1}{2}$ pint white or red
  grape juice
  concentrate 250 grams

$1\frac{3}{4}$ lb sugar   800 grams
6 pints water 3.5 litres
2 tsp. citric acid
$\frac{1}{2}$ tsp. tannin
Campden tablets
nutrient
Sauternes yeast

Make as for Recipe No. 141.

153 SUGAR BEET

4½ lb prepared sugar beet 2 kg
½ pint white grape juice concentrate 250 grams
1½ lb white sugar 700 grams

7 pints water 4 litres
¾ oz citric acid 20 grams
½ tsp. tannin
nutrient
G.P. yeast

1   Thoroughly scrub, clean and dice the sugar beet and simmer them in 7 pints (4 litres) water for 2 hours.
2   Strain on to the sugar, acid and tannin, and stir well.
3   When cool add the grape juice concentrate, nutrient and yeast.
4   Pour into a fermentation jar, top up, fit an air-lock and ferment out.

Note: This wine sometimes lacks flavour, but is excellent for blending, or in liqueurs. Other flavours may, of course, be added such as mint, peppermint, ginger, clove etc. Be gentle and add only a few drops at first. You can always add more. Liqueur essences may also be used.

154 SULTANA (dry)

3 lb 5 oz large seedless sultanas 1.5 kg
8 pints water 4.5 litres
2 tsp. citric acid

½ tsp. tannin
Campden tablets
nutrient
Hock yeast

Make as for Recipe No. 128.

155 SULTANA (sweet)

4 lb large seedless sultanas 1.8 kg
½ pint white grape juice concentrate 250 grams
7 pints water 4 litres

2 tsp. citric acid
½ tsp. tannin
Campden tablets
nutrient
Sauternes yeast

Make as for Recipe No. 128 but rack at S.G. 1.016 and add 2 crushed Campden tablets to terminate fermentation and leave the wine sweet.

156 TEA

12 tea bags
1 pint white grape juice
  concentrate 500 grams
2 lb sugar   900 grams
7 pints water   4 litres

3 tsp. citric acid
no tannin
Campden tablets
nutrient
G.P. yeast

1   Pour 5 pints (3 litres) boiling water on to the tea bags and stir well.
2   After 10 minutes remove the tea bags and stir in the sugar and acid. Cover and leave to cool.
3   Stir in the grape juice concentrate, nutrient and yeast.
4   Pour into a fermentation jar, top up, fit an air-lock and ferment to dryness or to S.G. 1.004 depending on your taste.

157 TOMATO

$5\frac{1}{2}$ lb very ripe tomatoes
       2.5 kg
$\frac{1}{2}$ pint white grape juice
  concentrate 250 grams
2 lb sugar   900 grams
6 pints water   3.5 litres

2 tsp. citric acid
$\frac{1}{2}$ tsp. tannin
Campden tablets
nutrient
G.P. yeast

1   Remove the stalks and wash the tomatoes, then mash them and pour on 5 pints (3 litres) boiling water.
2   When cool stir in the grape juice concentrate, acid, tannin, nutrient and yeast, and ferment for 5 days, stirring daily.
3   Strain out the solids, stir in the sugar, pour into a fermentation jar, top up, fit an air-lock and ferment to dryness.

158 TREE LEAF

N.B. Only oak and walnut are recommended

$2\frac{1}{4}$ lb young leaves
                              1 kg
$\frac{1}{2}$ pint white grape juice
    concentrate 250 grams
2 lb sugar   900 grams
7 pints water   4 litres

$\frac{1}{2}$ oz citric acid 15 grams
no tannin
Campden tablets
nutrient
G.P. yeast

1   Collect the leaves as soon as they are fully grown, rinse them in cold water in which a little citric acid and 1 Campden tablet have been dissolved. Strain and shake dry.
2   Pour on 5 pints (3 litres) boiling water and leave to cool.
3   Continue as for flower wines. See Recipe No. 42.

159 TREE SAP

N.B. Only birch, sycamore and walnut saps are recommended.

Take the sap only from mature trees in March in the following manner:

A   Bore a small hole 1″ (2.5 cm) deep, slanting upwards, about 15″ (40 cm) from the ground.

B   Push into the hole one end of a rubber tube and put the other end into a jar, the neck of which has been plugged round with cotton wool to keep out dust and insects.

C   Cover the jar to keep out the light and to protect the jar for 2 or 3 days until it is nearly full.

D   Plug the hole with a suitable cork to prevent further drainage and the death of the tree.

6 pints of sap   3.5 litres
½ pint white grape juice
  concentrate 250 grams
2¼ lb sugar   1 kg
2 tsp. citric acid

½ tsp. tannin
Campden tablets
nutrient
G.P. yeast

1. Simmer the sap, sugar and acid for 10 minutes.
2. When cool stir in the grape juice concentrate, tannin, nutrient and yeast.
3. Pour into a fermentation jar, top up, fit an air-lock and ferment to S.G. 1.008.
4. Rack and add 2 crushed Campden tablets to terminate fermentation so that this wine can be served slightly sweet.

160 VINE PRUNINGS OR FOLLY

5½ lb young vine
  prunings   2.5 kg
½ pint white grape juice
  concentrate 250 grams
2 lb sugar   900 grams
7 pints water   4 litres

2 tsp. citric acid
¼ tsp. tannin
pectic enzyme
Campden tablets
nutrient
Hock yeast

1. Wash the prunings and shake off the loose water, chop them small and place them in a mashing bin.
2. Pour on 5 pints (3 litres) boiling water and when cool add the acid, tannin, pectic enzyme and 1 Campden tablet. Cover and leave for 3 days, macerating the leaves thoroughly each day.
3. Strain and press the prunings, stir in the grape juice concentrate, sugar, nutrient and yeast.
4. Pour into a fermentation jar, top up, fit an air-lock and ferment out.

Note: Do NOT use leaves and tendrils that have previously been sprayed with Bordeaux Mixture (copper sulphate). These are poisonous.

161 WHEAT

1½ lb crushed wheat 700 grams
1 pint white grape juice concentrate 500 grams
18 oz sugar 500 grams
6 pints water 3.5 litres

½ oz citric acid 15 grams
½ tsp. tannin
Campden tablets
nutrient
Cereal yeast

1. Wash the crushed wheat free from dust and pour on 5 pints (3 litres) boiling water. Stir in the sugar, acid and tannin.
2. When cool stir in the grape juice concentrate, nutrient and yeast. Ferment for 5 days, stirring twice daily.
3. Strain out the wheat, pour into a fermentation jar, top up, fit an air-lock and ferment to S.G. 1.020.
4. Rack and add 2 crushed Campden tablets to terminate fermentation, so that the wine can be served sweet.

162 WHITE CURRANTS

3 lb 5 oz fresh white currants 1.5 kg
½ pint white grape juice concentrate 250 grams
2 lb white sugar 900 grams
6 pints water 3.5 litres

½ tsp. tannin
pectic enzyme
Campden tablets
nutrient
Chablis yeast
No acid is required

Make as for Recipe No. 131.

163 WHORTLEBERRY

The Bilberry is known in some places as the Blueberry and in others as the Whortleberry. The wine is prepared in the same way whatever name is used. See Recipes 21 and 22.

Brewing Beer at Home

Beer is traditionally the Englishman's drink and Englishmen have been drinking it for a very long time indeed. Brewing beer at home is a totally successful and rewarding endeavour. The average amateur winemaker can usually produce excellent quality "vin ordinaire" and sometimes something even better. The very best amateur winemaker however, is quite unable to make wines comparable with the very best French wines. With brewing beer at home, the situation is reversed. Sometimes with your first brew, and certainly after a little experience, it is easily possible to brew a very much better beer than you can buy. It is usually superior in body, in bouquet and in flavour and is certainly very much more satisfying. A glass or two of a well made home-brewed beer is enough for the vast majority of men and women. There is simply no question of drinking three or four pints, or more!

Beer is extremely easy to brew at home and has the great advantage that it matures much more quickly, and yet really superb beers may be kept for up to a year.

History

The drink that we call "beer" today was originally called "ale". It was a word in such common use that it was added to many other words to widen their description, e.g. alehouse — a place where ale was brewed and sold. Alewife — a woman who brewed ale, and so on.

At first an ale was made by fermenting an extract from cereals or grains. Wheat and rye was used as well as barley and in those parts of the world where maize is grown it was frequently used instead, especially in Africa. Herbs of one kind or another were used for flavouring but the favourite was the ordinary stinging nettle. Self-supporting families made their own ale for their own use. Estate workers received free ale as part of their wages. As communications developed and taverns came into existence each one brewed their own ale and put a fresh bush outside their house to indicate that they had just brewed a vat or tun of ale.

Although the Romans had imported hops to flavour their own beer, the taste never really caught on with our forebears for more than a thousand years. Hopped ale which we now call beer did not come into common use until the beginning of the 15th century and by this time there was a "London Guild of Brewers" to control the making of beers for sale, even though it had been made commercially for 200 years or so before this.

Throughout the country ale and beer was the drink of the common people, prior to the introduction of tea, coffee, cocoa, and so on in the eighteenth century. In many places the water was impure and sometimes even contaminated, through inadequate or non-existent sewers. In the making of beer the contents have to be boiled and this at least purified the water. A drink called "small-beer" which was often given to the children or drunk at breakfast by the very poor, had little body or flavouring and was only slightly alcoholic. Better qualities of beer were drunk at other times of the day however, especially for the evening meal at the end of a hard day's work. There was a constant search for improvement in quality and flavour and frequently different kinds of beers were blended together. The most popular for a period was called "porter beer" which was simply a blend of stout and the ordinary mild ale of the day. It received its name because it was drunk by the London porters who found the stout alone too heavy.

Facilities available

It is easier to brew beer at home today than ever before. The ingredients are very readily available in every town. The malt can be bought either as grains, as malt flour, as malt extract in a jar or as a prepared hopped malt extract requiring only sugar, water and yeast. These are all pre-

Beer tastes even better with the right foods.

pared specially for the home-brewer. Hops can be bought in small quantities and of different varieties for different purposes. Lager yeast can be bought as well as the ordinary granulated beer yeast. Indeed, frequently, fresh brewer's yeast can be readily obtained. Although you may be living in a soft water area, the water can be hardened and likened to that of the mineral spring water of Burton on Trent by the addition of hardening salts. For those who wish to imitate the commercial process precisely, one can buy water heaters and thermostats as well as sparging facilities. Vessels of miniature sizes holding one, two and three gallons (and 10, 15 and 25 litres) can be bought inexpensively. A simple crown corking device has been produced for capping bottles at home. There are also carbonating devices available for those who wish to brew draught beer in a keg and draw from it when they want to.

No licence is required to brew beer at home, although prior to 1963 this was the case. However, it is illegal to sell home-brewed beer without a licence, but then who would want to!

Serving Beer

When bottled beer has matured there will be a thin deposit on the bottom of the bottle. When serving care must be taken not to disturb this sediment. Before the crown cork is removed or the stopper unscrewed, the glasses should be placed ready in position. When the bottle is opened there will be a rush of carbon dioxide trying to escape and this will tend to lift the sediment off the bottom. Care should therefore be taken to pour the beer as quickly as possible down the side of the glasses one after another so that the bottle does not have to be tilted back and forth. This is a very simple matter and the bottle can be emptied to within half an inch of the bottom. The beer will be found to have plenty of life, a good head, an attractive bouquet with a satisfying body and texture. It is possible to remove the beer from the sediment by chilling it down to a temperature of 34° to 36°F (1° or 2°C) before carefully siphoning off the clear beer into a clean bottle and replacing the stopper or cap.

Priming, i.e. the addition of sugar in the bottle to cause a secondary fermentation, is of the utmost importance. Too little priming sugar and the beer will have insufficient life and head and will quickly become flat in the glass. Too much sugar will cause the enormous rush of escaping carbon dioxide to lift the sediment off the bottom and carry it to the top the moment the bottle is opened and then into the glass.

Malt flour may be used instead of malt extract in any of the recipes but the result is not as satisfying for the author as the malt extract that looks like toffee.

Malt

By the 14th century the process of malting barley had become quite common and barley had established itself as the most suitable grain or cereal for making ale or beer.

Traditionally the process of malting barley has been a separate occupation. Briefly, the process was and fundamentally still is, to soak the grains in water until they start to swell and then to store them in a warm place for a few days until they begin to sprout. This process converts the starch into sugar that can be fermented. Starch cannot be fermented directly into sugar and an enzyme in the barley grain called diastase, in the wet warm conditions created by the maltster, converts the starch into maltose, a simple sugar that can be converted by another enzyme called maltase, into the fructose and glucose necessary for the fermentation by the apo-zymase complex of enzymes into alcohol. After the starch has been converted into sugar, the grains are roasted to prevent further growth and to vary the flavour. The grains are only lightly roasted for light ales and bitters, more thoroughly roasted until the grains are almost black for stout.

Malting is now a highly scientific process in which a very precise quantity of water is used and the temperature is maintained at a constant figure for a very precise period of time. This ensures a constant standard of malt, not subject to wide variations. On the other hand barley is

162

grown in different parts of the country and in varying conditions, so in fact the flavour and quality does vary subtly and, as with all other products, some are better than others. The great care taken in the process of malting, however, ensures that the minimum standard is as high as possible.

Hops

These are the dried flowers of the hop-vine. They are greeny-yellow, about the size of a large gooseberry and consist of overlapping petals. They impart to the beer that special bitter flavour as well as assist in protecting it from infection. Although there are a number of hops available, the most popular varieties are Fuggles, used primarily for mild ales, brown ales and stouts, and Goldings used for bitter beers, pale ales and lager type beers. Hallertau, the true lager hop, is not grown in Great Britain. 1– 2 oz of hops per 2 gallons (30 – 60 grams per 9 litres) is usually sufficient for the different types of beer but the actual quantity you use depends entirely on your own palate.

Washings

The water in which you have rinsed off the maltings from the grains.

Water

The main ingredient of ale and beer is water and it soon became evident to intelligent brewers and travellers that beers made in one place, differed in flavour from those made in another. Spring water varies in its mineral content quite considerably, and different towns became famous for different beers, depending on the quality of the water available in their neighbourhood. Burton on Trent for example became famous for its light ales, due to the high mineral content of the water from its springs, which give its beers a clean crisp flavour. At the other end of the scale London became famous for its stout because the water bubbling up through its clay contains fewer minerals and is very much softer. This gives a smooth finish to this very popular black beer.

Making Beer Step by Step

1. USING HOPPED MALT EXTRACT

1 a. Pour the hopped malt extract into warm water

1 b. Add sugar and stir well

2. USING A DRY INGREDIENTS KIT

2 a. Boil the hops and grain

2 b. Pour the liquor onto the sugar and malt flour

CONTINUE FOR BOTH 1 AND 2

c. Top up and check the temperature

d. Pitch the yeast at 60°F. (15°C.)

e. Fermentation in progress

f. Fermentation finished

g. Check the specific gravity

h. Siphon into beer bottles and add primer.

i. Hammer on crown caps

j. Ready for drinking on the left. A flat beer on the right. (Bottle not airtight or priming sugar omitted.)

Yeast

Brewer's yeast is the variety Saccharomyces Cerevisae. It is circular in shape and ferments very rapidly. It is usually supplied to the home-brewer in granulated form and should be activated before use. Half a pint (a quarter litre) of a thin solution of malt extract is a suitable base in which to activate the yeast. It will take only half an hour to prepare for pitching into the main wort. For lager a special yeast called Saccharomyces Carlsbergensis should be used to ensure the correct fermentation and flavour.

Nutrient

Although malt contains nutrients of its own, it is customary to include a little extra nutrient to ensure a quick and efficient fermentation. Often a sachet of granulated beer yeast will include a sufficient nutrient consisting of di-ammonium phosphate, vitamin B1 and citric acid. If it does not, a half teaspoonful of beer nutrient per 2 gallons (9 litres) of beer should be added when pitching the yeast.

Acid

Similarly malt contains certain acids sufficient for fermentation but a small quantity of citric acid aids fermentation. This too is often included in a sachet of yeast but if not, then half a teaspoonful per 2 gallons (9 litres) is sufficient.

Sugar

To ensure a very rapid fermentation commercial brewers use invert sugar to increase the alcoholic strength of their beer. The home-brewer may use this sugar or ordinary white granulated sugar, or for dark beers demerera or soft brown sugar. The sugar may be added in granule form or better still in syrup form. 2 lb (1 kg) of sugar and $\frac{1}{2}$ teaspoonful of citric acid gently boiled in a pint (half a litre) of water for 10 minutes makes an excellent sugar syrup for brewing. The purpose of the sugar is to obtain additional alcohol cheaply, since malt is quite expensive; nevertheless, to use too much sugar diminishes the malty flavour of beer and causes it to taste rather thin. A reasonable proportion is 2 measures of malt to 1 of sugar.

Finings

Beer usually clears naturally, but to quicken the process it is now customary to add gelatine finings. This greatly benefits both bottled and draught beer and minimises the residual deposit after priming. Many beer packs on the market include a packet of finings as well as a composite packet of yeast granules, nutrient and acid.

Beer Kits

Ready-prepared packs to make 8 to 40 bottles of beer are readily available with step by step advice on how to brew beer from them. Some packs however, produce a somewhat thin beer upon which one can make individual improvements. The taste for beer is a very personal matter, and a few experiments will soon enable you to produce one that tastes the way you like it. You have only to adjust the quantities of malt or sugar or hops sufficiently to suit your palate. Basic recipes follow for beers from packs, for beers from malt extract, hops and grains and finally for brewing beer at home from grains, hops and sugar alone.

Basic recipe for brewing 16 pints (9 litres) bitter beer from a can of hopped malt extract.

1 Place 1 quart (1 litre) of water in an aluminium or stainless steel saucepan and bring it to the boil.
2 Open the can of hopped malt extract, pour the contents into the saucepan, stirring gently till the malt is dissolved. Pour some of the hot wort back into the can and stir well, to ensure that all the malt extract is dissolved and poured into the saucepan.
3 Stir in 12 oz (340 grams) of granulated white sugar.
4 When all is dissolved, bring to the boil and simmer gently for five minutes.
5 Pour 1 gallon (5 litres) of cold water into a polythene bin large enough to hold 3 gallons (15 litres).
6 Pour the hot wort into the bin and then add sufficient cold water – about 4 pints (2 litres) to bring the total up to 1 gallon (9 litres).
7 Stir in the yeast provided, cover the vessel with the lid of the bin, a clean tea towel or similar cloth.

8 Stand the bin in a warm place 65° to 70°F (18° to 20°C) for 5 to 7 days until fermentation is complete i.e. when no bubbles rise to the surface. The S.G. should be down to about 1.000 but may occassionally be higher depending on the amount of unfermentable sugar included in the malt to give body to the beer. DO NOT BOTTLE IF IT IS 1.008 OR MORE.

9 Finings should now be stirred in and the beer left for 2 days in a cool place to clear.

10 Siphon or pour the beer into prepared beer bottles, or a pressure barrel, being careful not to disturb the sediment on the bottom of the bin.

11 Fill the bottles to within 2" (5 cm) of the top and to every 1 pint bottle (approx half litre) add half a teaspoonful of granulated white sugar.

12 Crown cap the bottles or screw in the stoppers. Shake the bottle gently to dissolve the sugar and leave them in a warm room for 7 days.

13 Remove the bottles to a cool place and store for a few days or, better still, weeks, before drinking the beer.

14 Instead of bottling a pressure barrel may be used. Precise instructions are given with each barrel and vary slightly between manufacturers.

Priming is at the rate of about $\frac{1}{2}$ oz (15 grams) per 1 gallon (4.5 litres). When pressure falls the beer must be reprimed at the same rate.

If a CO_2 injector is incorporated in your pressure barrel, priming at this rate is still important and the first 2 gallons (9 litres) of a 5 gallon (25 litres) barrel may be drawn off naturally. CO_2 is then injected to raise the pressure to the level prescribed by the manufacturers and the beer can be drawn off again as required.

A pressure barrel is a great advantage when brewing 4 – 5 gallons (20 – 25 litres) of your favourite beer every few weeks. It saves a lot of time washing and sterilising 40 bottles, filling them one by one, priming each one separately and then capping, labelling and handling.

On the other hand bottled beer can be matured more effectively and a wider range of beers can be made and stored in this way, unless you invest in a range of pressure barrels each for a different type of beer.

A combination of processes is the ideal for the serious home brewer. Pressure barrel for every day drinking, bottled beer for special types.

These beers do improve with keeping for a few weeks.

Cans of prepared malt extract are available to make lager, light ale, mild ale, brown ale, pale ale, bitter beer and stout. All ingredients are provided except sugar and water. Make-up time takes only a few minutes, equipment is minimal, satisfaction is assured — if you give the beer time to mature!

Basic recipe for brewing 16 pints (9 litres) beer from malt extract and hops.

$2\frac{1}{4}$ lb Boots extract of malt   1 kg

2 oz hops (Fuggles or Goldings)   60 grams

1 lb granulated white sugar   500 grams

12 pints water (approx.)   7 litres

Juice of half a lemon

a pinch of salt

2 tsp. granulated brewing yeast

1 Place 4 pints (2 litres) of water in a large saucepan or preserving pan and bring to the boil.
2 Add the sugar, salt, malt extract and stir till thoroughly dissolved.
3 Place all but a handful of hops into the pan and press them down with a wooden spoon until they are thoroughly wet.
4 Bring to the boil and continue boiling vigorously for $\frac{3}{4}$ hour, then remove from the heat.
5 Strain out the hops and pour the beer into a fermentation bin. Add sufficient cold water to make up to 16 pints (9 litres).

6 Stir in the remaining handful of fresh hops, the lemon juice and an active beer yeast. Cover the vessel and leave in a warm place for 3 days.

7 On the 3rd day skim off the dirty froth, re-cover and leave for 2 more days.

8 On the 5th day stir the beer well and move the bin to a cool place for 2 days while the sediment settles.

9 Carefully siphon or pour the beer into bottles without disturbing the thick paste of sandy coloured sediment. Fill the bottles to within 2" (5 cm) of the top.

10 Prime each bottle with $\frac{1}{2}$ teaspoonful of sugar to the pint (half litre).

11 Cap the bottles or screw in the stoppers and leave them in a warm place for the priming sugar to ferment.

12 Store the bottles in a cool place for at least two weeks before drinking the beer.

VARIATIONS

MILD BEER

2 lb Boots malt extract
1 kg

1½ oz hops (Fuggles for preference)
45 grams

14 pints water (approx.)
8 litres

2 tsp. granulated beer yeast

Method as for basic beer, page 169.
Note: This is a weak beer ready for drinking 1 week after bottling and does not keep more than three months.

STRONG BEER

2 lb Boots malt extract
            1 kg
2 lb crystal malt grains
            1 kg
2 lb soft brown sugar
         900 grams
3 oz hops   85 grams

Juice only of half a
   lemon
¼ tsp. of table salt
12 pints water (approx.)
         7 litres
2 tsp. granulated
   beer yeast

As for basic recipe. Include all the grains with the hops for boiling.
Starting S.G. should be about 1.055.
This beer needs at least 3 weeks to mature and will certainly improve if kept for 3 months.

BITTER BEER

1 lb Boots malt extract
       500 grams
1 lb crystal malt grains
       500 grams
1 lb Golden syrup
       500 grams
3 oz hops (Golding for
 preference) 85 grams

Juice of half a lemon
Hardening salts (quantity
   to use will be indicated
   by manufacturer)
14 pints water (approx.)
        8 litres
2 tsp. granulated
   beer yeast

As for basic recipe. Include the Golden Syrup in place of the sugar and the hardening salts in place of the table salt.
Starting S.G. should be about 1.040.

BROWN ALE

2 lb Boots malt extract
            1 kg
4 oz black malt grains
       100 grams
1 lb soft brown sugar
       430 grams
2 oz hops (Fuggles for

   preference) 50 grams
Juice only of half a lemon
¼ tsp. table salt
14 pints water (approx.)
        8 litres
2 tsp. granulated
   beer yeast

As for basic recipe. If soft water is used salt may be omitted.

A selection of beer bottles, caps and labels. The capping tool is being hit with a specially designed dead head hammer. The seal must be strong and air tight under pressure.

A wide selection of beer kits and equipment. In the background a pressure cask for beer 'on tap'.

STOUT

2 lb Boots extract
of malt   1 kg
9 oz black malt grains
                250 grams
26 oz soft brown sugar
                750 grams

Juice only of half a lemon
¼ tsp. of table salt
14 pints water (approx.)
                8 litres
2 tsp. granulated
beer yeast

As for basic recipe. If soft water is used salt may be omitted.

MILK STOUT

For those who like a sweeter taste to their stout ½ lb (250 grams) lactose (milk sugar) may be added to the ingredients for stout. Lactose cannot be fermented by beer yeast and so remains in solution giving a slightly milky, sweeter taste to the beer. The quantity used may be varied to suit your palate. It should be added with the malt extract.

BREWING BEER FROM GRAINS

Beer is made by soaking malt grains in water at 150°F (65.6°C) for about 6 hours and then this liquor is drained off whilst fresh hot water of the same temperature is slowly sprayed on to the top of the grains for the next half hour. As this soaks through to the bottom outlet of the vessel in which the grains have been soaking, the water steadily extracts all the fermentable sugars and proteins. This liquid, now called the wort, is placed in the special boiler and together with hops, is boiled vigorously for an hour to extract the hop oils and flavours and to pasteurise the wort. The liquor is then strained off and cooled quite rapidly to 65°F (18.3°C) so that an active beer yeast can be added and fermentation started without delay. A frothy head soon appears on the wort and after a few days this changes in character and colour and is skimmed off. A few days later the new beer is filtered and poured into casks and additional hops and sugar called priming are

174

added. The cask is bunged tight and allowed to stand for a few days before being distributed to public-houses. Here it is again allowed to stand for a few days so that the hops and yeast can settle. The beer is then drawn off clear and bright and with a good head. Some brewers are now by-passing this latter process by sending out their beers flat in steel containers. The beer is then carbonated as it is drawn off. Clearly this has certain advantages over the older methods and the condition of the beer can be more accurately controlled.

With the aid of a water heater of the kind used in the home aquarium together with a thermostat this process can be imitated quite closely at home. The malt grains and water are poured into a polythene bin-like container, the water heater and thermostat are put in, connected to the electricity mains and switched on, the thermostat being regulated to operate at 150°F (65.6°C). Some hours later the wort is strained off the grain, hops are added and the whole is boiled for an hour, then strained and cooled before the yeast is added in an active liquid form. Fermentation starts almost at once. Two or three days later the scum is skimmed off and after 5 days or so the beer is ready to be fined, bottled, primed and stored or transferred in a plastic pressure barrel to become a draft beer.

Undoubtedly this method produces the best beers especially after a few brews when the technique has been mastered. The following basic recipe for a light ale may be varied by using different or blended malt grains, adding different adjuncts, e.g., flaked oats, wheat, rice and so on.

Assorted beers The lager is cloudy due to the yeast rising when the bottle was tilted upright between pouring the first glass and the second.

LIGHT ALE

3 lb 5 oz crushed pale
malt barley   1.5 kg

4½ oz flaked maize
       125 grams

7 oz granulated sugar
       200 grams

1¾ oz hops (Golding
for preference)
       50 grams

2 gallons water   9 litres

Sachet of Beer yeast,
nutrient and acid

1 Heat 1¾ gallons (8 litres) of water to 158°F (70°C), add the crushed malt grains, maize and sugar, stir to dissolve the sugar and check the temperature. If necessary adjust to 152°F (66°C). Temperature is critical and variation of a degree or two will alter the extract.

2 Maintain this temperature for 15 minutes, then stir well to assist extraction.

3 Leave for 30 minutes at the same temperature of 152°F (66°C) then stir well once more.

4 Leave for a further 15 minutes still at 152°F (66°C).

5 Strain off all the liquor and wash the grains with 2 pints (1 litre) of hot water – 158°F (70°C), to ensure that all the maltose extract is removed. Add the washings to the liquor.

6 Add the hops to the liquor and boil vigorously for ¾ hour to extract the hop oils and coagulate the proteins in the liquor.

7 Strain the liquor through the hops into a fermentation vessel. Wash the hops in 1 pint (½ litre) of warm water and cool all the liquor as quickly as possible.

8 As soon as the temperature reaches 59°F (15°C) check the S.G. and adjust if necessary, either by dilution with cold boiled water or by the addition of sugar syrup, to between 1.038 and 1.042.

9 Stir in an active beer yeast and ferment at this temperature for 2 days. Remove the yeast head, re-cover the vessel and continue fermentation to the end.

10 Give the beer a good stir to remove any remaining carbon dioxide, add some beer finings and leave the beer in a cool place for 3 days for the sediment to

settle.

11 Rack into sterile bottles, prime, stopper and label. Leave in a warm room for 2 days for the secondary fermentation, then store for 3 weeks at least.

How to Make Mead

This once common and popular beverage is slowly coming back into fashion again. It is probably the oldest fermented drink known to mankind and is thought to have been drunk some 12,000 years ago. Until sugar became widely and cheaply available honey was the only source of sweetening and there is no doubt that many rough wines were made more palatable by the admixture of some honey.

With the advent of sugar and the flight from the land at the time of the industrial revolution, the keeping of bees declined and so disappeared the source of cheap honey. British honey is in fact still in short supply and therefore relatively expensive. Happily good quality imported honey can be bought for a reasonable price, especially if it is bought in bulk.

The creamy white honey is best for making mead, since it possesses a more subtle flavour. The brown honey is of a much stronger flavour and is best used with herbs and spices. Australian blended honey sometimes contains nectar from the eucalyptus tree and has a pungent bitterness that is best avoided.

Mead is something of an acquired taste, perhaps, but for those who like the flavour it is a beneficial and health-giving drink. It is clean and easy to make and can often be drunk whilst still quite young, especially mead made from the flower blossom honeys. Sometimes, however, it is slow to ferment and takes as long as six months to finish and will then take two or three years to mature. Mead blends well, not only with other wines, but also with fruit juices and herbs. It can be served chilled and dry at table strength with fish or chicken or sweeter with the dessert course.

Unfortunately honey contains neither acid nor tannin. Nor indeed is there any nitrogenous matter to serve as nutrient for yeast. These ingredients must necessarily always be added. Just for the record honey consists of :— 77% sugar, $17\frac{1}{2}$% water, the remaining $5\frac{1}{2}$% includes salts of iron, phosphorus, lime, sodium, potassium sulphate and manganese with traces of citric, formic, malic, succinic, and amino acids together with dextrin, pollen, oils, gums, waxes, fats, yeast enzymes, vitamins, albumen, protein and ash.

Any wine yeast will ferment a honey solution containing acid and nutrient, but practical experience shows that Maury yeast gives the best results followed by a Sherry yeast, and a general purpose wine yeast.

The method of making mead is similar to that of making wine from grape juice concentrate.

TABLE MEAD (dry)

$3\frac{1}{4}$ lb white honey such as clover   1.5 kg
6 pints water   3.5 litres
$\frac{1}{2}$ oz citric acid   15 grams

Campden tablets
nutrient
Maury yeast

1   Warm the water and dissolve the honey in it.
2   When cool pour the honey solution into a jar together with the acid, nutrient and yeast.
3   Top up the jar with cold boiled water, fit an air-lock and ferment to dryness.
4   Rack into a clean jar, add 1 Campden tablet and store to mature – about a year.

TABLE MEAD
(sweet)

3½ lb white honey such as imported orange blossom   1.6 kg
6 pints water   3.5 litres
½ oz citric acid 15 grams

¼ oz malic acid 7 grams
¼ tsp. tannin
Campden tablets
nutrient
Sauternes yeast

1   Warm the water and dissolve the honey in it.
2   When cool pour the honey solution into a jar with the acids, tannin, nutrient and yeast.
3   Top up the jar with cold boiled water, fit an air-lock and ferment to S.G. 1.010.
4   Rack into a clean jar, add 2 crushed Campden tablets, and store.

HEATHER HONEY

3¼ lb heather honey   1.5 kg
6 pints water   3.5 litres
¼ oz each citric, tartaric and malic acids   7 grams each

¼ tsp. tannin
Campden tablets
nutrient
Madeira yeast

This is a strongly flavoured, slow maturing mead but well worth making.
Make as for a sweet mead.

MELOMEL I
Honey and fruit juices

2¼ lb honey   1.5 kg
3½ oz blackcurrants
     100 grams
7 oz redcurrants
     200 grams

7 oz small green
   gooseberries 200 grams
6 pints water   3.5 litres
Campden tablets
nutrient
Bordeaux yeast

1   Dissolve the honey in warm water.
2   Wash and stalk the fruit, crush it and stir it into the honey solution.
3   Add 1 crushed Campden tablet as soon as the mixture is cool.
4   Cover and leave for 24 hours.
5   Stir in the nutrient, tannin and yeast.
6   Ferment in a warm place for 7 days.
7   Strain out the fruit, pour the must into a fermentation jar, top up with cold boiled water and continue fermentation to S.G. 1.006.
8   Rack into a clean jar, add 2 crushed Campden tablets, and store.

MELOMEL II
(sweet)

3½ lb honey   1.6 kg
½ pint white grape juice
   concentrate 250 grams
6 Seville oranges
6 sugar lumps
6 pints water   3.5 litres

1 tsp. tartaric or malic
  acid
¼ tsp. tannin
Campden tablets
nutrient
Sauternes yeast

1   Dissolve the grape juice concentrate and honey in warm water.
2   Wash and dry the oranges and rub each one all over with a lump of sugar to extract the zest.
3   Cut the oranges in half and express the juice.
4   Add the orange juice and sugar lumps to the must, together with the acid, tannin, nutrient and an active yeast.
5   Pour into a fermentation jar, top up with cold boiled

water, fit an air-lock and ferment in a warm place to S.G. 1.020.

6   Rack into a clean jar, add 2 Campden tablets to terminate fermentation, then store.

SPARKLING MEAD

3¼ lb flower blossom honey   1.5 kg
6 pints water   3.5 litres
½ oz citric acid
           15 grams

¼ tsp. tannin
Campden tablets
nutrient
Champagne yeast

1   Prepare as for a dry mead.
2   When mead is 6 months old siphon into Champagne bottles.
3   Dissolve 2 oz (60 grams) of white honey in 3 fl oz (60 ml) of active Champagne yeast from a starter bottle and distribute evenly between the 6 bottles.
4   Stopper tightly, leave in a warm place for 7 days, then store in the cool.

CYSER (dry)

2¼ lb honey   1 kg
3½ pints apple juice
           2 litres
3½ pints water   2 litres
2 tsp. citric acid

¼ tsp. tannin
Campden tablets
nutrient
Maury yeast

1   Use a blend of cooking, crab and dessert apples or bottles of pure apple juice from the supermarket.
2   Dissolve the honey in warm water and when cool stir in the apple juice, acid, tannin, nutrient and yeast. Pour into a fermentation jar, top up with cold boiled water, fit an air-lock and ferment in a warm place to dryness.
3   Rack into a clean jar, add 1 crushed Campden tablet, then store.

CYSER (sweet)

2¼ lb honey   1 kg
3½ pints apple juice
    2 litres
½ pint white grape juice
    concentrate
    250 grams

3 pints water 1.75 litres
2 tsp. citric acid
¼ tsp. tannin
Campden tablets
nutrient
Sauternes yeast

Make as for a sweet mead.

PYMENT I
(dry white)
Honey and grape juice

2¼ lb white flower
    blossom honey 1 kg
1 pint white grape juice
    concentrate
    500 grams
6 pints water 3.5 litres

2 tsp. citric acid
¼ tsp. tannin
Campden tablets
nutrient
Hock yeast

Make as for a dry mead.

PYMENT II
(dry red)

2¼ lb blended brown
    honey   1 kg
1 pint red grape juice
    concentrate 500 grams
6 pints water 3.5 litres

2 tsp. citric acid
¼ tsp. tannin
Campden tablets
nutrient
Bordeaux yeast

Make as for a dry mead.

PYMENT III
(sweet red)

2¼ lb blended brown
    honey   1 kg
1 pint red grape juice
    concentrate 500 grams
7 oz soft brown sugar
    200 grams

6 pints water 3.5 litres
2 tsp. citric acid
¼ tsp. tannin
Campden tablets
nutrient
Madeira yeast

Make as for a sweet mead.

184

METHEGLIN I

This is a strongly flavoured and spiced mead.

3¼ lb blended honey — brown may be used
    1.5 kg
6 pints water   3.5 litres
7 oz Demerara sugar
    200 grams

Thinly pared rind of a lemon
¾ oz citric acid 21 grams
Campden tablets
nutrient
Sauternes yeast

Also bouquet garni of mixed herbs such as balm, rosemary, mace etc., using as many as possible so that no single flavour predominates.

1　Warm the water and dissolve the honey in it.
2　When cool pour the honey solution into a jar together with the sugar, acid, nutrient and yeast.
3　Tie the herbs and thinly pared lemon rind into a muslin bag and suspend them in the jar for the first 7 days of fermentation.
4　Remove the muslin bag and continue fermentation to S.G. 1.020.
5　Rack into a clean jar and add 2 crushed Campden tablets to terminate fermentation.
6　Store for at least 1 year in jar and 1 year in bottle.

METHEGLIN II

Make exactly as the first Metheglin but use . . .

½ oz crushed root ginger   15 grams
12 whole cloves, and

1 small stick of cinnamon
instead of the herbs.

Note : Metheglin must be served sweet. It is not attractive as a dry mead.

HYPOCRAS I
Spiced grape
wine and honey

2¼ lb honey   1 kg
1 pint white grape juice
  concentrate 500 grams
6 pints water   3.5 litres
Bouquet garni of balm
  rosemary, marjoram etc.

Rind only of 1 lemon
2 tsp. citric acid
¼ tsp. tannin
Campden tablets
nutrient
Sauternes yeast

Make as for Metheglin I.

HYPOCRAS II

2¼ lb blended brown
  honey   1 kg
1 pint red grape juice
  concentrate 500 grams
6 pints water   3.5 litres
¼ oz bruised root
  ginger   10 grams

6 whole cloves
2 tsp. citric acid
¼ tsp. tannin
Campden tablets
nutrient
Sauternes yeast

Make as for Metheglin I.

Note: Hypocras must be served sweet. If it is not sweet enough for your palate sweeten it just before serving either with honey or sugar.

Liqueurs

A liqueur is usually a very strong, sweet, highly flavoured beverage, taken in a small quantity after a meal. Just as an aperitif stimulates the gastric juices before a meal, so a liqueur relaxes them after a meal.

There are several kinds of liqueurs.

1   The distillation of fruit wines to produce a fruit brandy. The best known example of this is Calvados made from the spirit obtained from a distillation of a fermented apple juice.

2   The marinading of fruit in a spirit. A suitable example is Sloe Gin. The fruit is cleaned and pricked and left in the spirit for some months so that its colour and flavour is leached out by the alcohol.

3   The fruit essence is mixed with spirit. This is often done for manufacturing simplicity and some of the cheaper liqueurs are so made.

4   In addition to fruits, herbs, beans and spices are sometimes used. Tia Maria for example is a coffee flavoured rum.

It is quite properly illegal to distil spirits in any way in the home or without a licence. Special knowledge is required and if distillation is not properly done, great harm, including death, could result from drinking the imperfect spirit.

At home we can make excellent liqueurs by marinading fruit in spirits and by adding essences to spirit, wine and sugar. These are quite excellent imitations of the real liqueurs and costing less than half as much.

It is not essential to make liqueurs of very high alcoholic content and a strong wine can successfully take the place of some of the spirit. A liqueur of 31° Proof is most attractive and costs only one third the price of the original. Many liqueur flavourings are widely available and precise details come with each one but they need to be followed with a certain caution.

Ingredients are simply spirit, wine, sugar and flavouring. The only equipment required is a clean bottle and a cork stopper. A jug and spoon are desirable but not absolutely essential.

For most liqueurs Vodka is the recommended spirit because it is colourless and flavourless. It is customarily available at 65.5° Proof, but can also be obtained at twice the strength, as Polish Spirit.

Ordinary white granulated sugar is the best to use if possible. A strong wine of similar colour to the finished liqueur is needed. White or golden wines are mostly used but a red wine is required for Cherry Brandy and the like. Grape juice concentrate wines fermented on with extra sugar make an excellent base for this purpose. Spanish Sauterne is equally good. The flavourings vary in quality and after some experiment you will find that you like certain varieties from one manufacturer and others from another.

Usually flavourings are too strong. Where it is recommended to use the whole bottle of essence in the making of one full bottle of liqueur, start off by using only a half to two thirds. If upon tasting the final result you feel that the flavour is not quite strong enough, then you can always add a little more essence. It is not possible to remove an excess of flavour except by dilution, and this is rarely satisfactory.

Similarly with sugar. Start off with two thirds of the recommended quantity say 6 oz (170 grams) instead of 9 oz (255 grams) in a bottle. If the result is not sweet enough for your palate you can always add a little more but too much sugar spoils the balance.

All you have to do is to mix all the ingredients together and leave it for a few days to homogenize. The following example produces an extremely pleasant and warming, liqueur type drink of about 31° Proof.

14 fl oz (400 ml) **strong white wine**

7 fl oz (200 ml) **Vodka (65.5° Proof)**

6 oz (170 grams) **white sugar**

$\frac{2}{3}$ **bottle Apricot Brandy Liqueur Flavouring**

A variety of different flavourings are available in larger branches of Boots and are well worth making. The liqueur is ready for drinking in a week and a bottle lasts quite a long while. It is worth making up at least 4 different liqueurs at a time. Use a large bottle of Vodka, two bottles of wine and $1\frac{1}{2}$ lb (680 grams) of sugar. It takes only minutes to dissolve the sugar in the Vodka and wine, pour it into 4 bottles and add a different flavouring to each. Fit a good stopper, stick on a label, give each bottle a good shake and there you are. Drink it slowly after meals!

Index